Engaging

Every

Learner

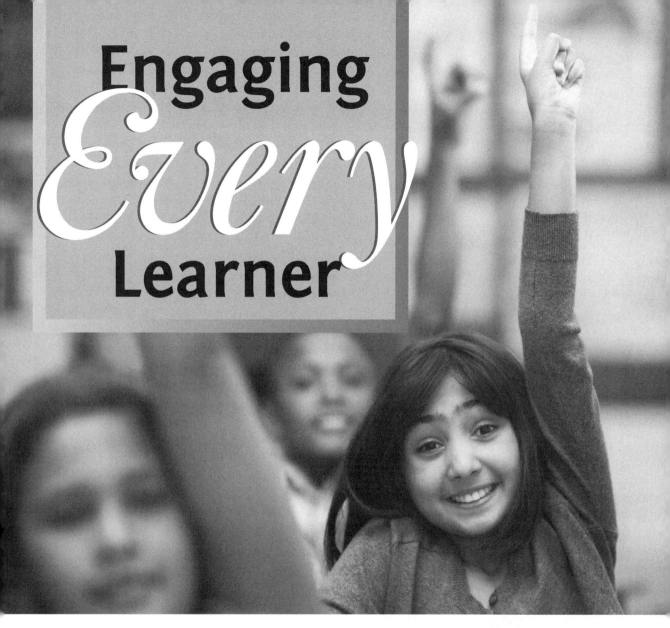

Engaging *Every* Learner

Classroom Principles, Strategies, and Tools

Patricia Vitale-Reilly

HEINEMANN
Portsmouth, NH

Heinemann
361 Hanover Street
Portsmouth, NH 03801–3912
www.heinemann.com

Offices and agents throughout the world

The author and publisher wish to thank those who have generously given permission to reprint borrowed material:

Figure 1.2a: Adapted from *Notice and Note: Strategies for Close Reading* by Kylene Beers and Robert E. Probst. Copyright © 2013 by Kylene Beers and Robert E. Probst. Published by Heinemann, Portsmouth, NH. All rights reserved.

Figure 1.3: Classroom Architect from 4Teachers.org. Copyright © 2000–2008 by ALTEC at the University of Kansas Center for Research on Learning. Used with permission.

Figure 6.1: From Kahoot! A Game-based Classroom Response System, getkahoot.com. Copyright Kahoot! 2014. Used with permission.

Library of Congress Cataloging-in-Publication Data

Vitale-Reilly, Patricia.
    Engaging every learner : classroom principles, strategies, and tools / Patricia Vitale-Reilly.
        pages cm
    Includes bibliographical references.
    ISBN 978-0-325-06290-7
    1. Effective teaching. 2. Teaching—Evaluation. 3. Learning. 4. Learning, Psychology of.
5. Classroom management. I. Title.
LB1025.3.V59 2015
371.102—dc23   2014046264

Editor: Holly Kim Price
Development editor: Alan Huisman
Production: Hilary Goff
Cover and interior designs: Monica Ann Crigler
Cover image: Peopleimages.com / Getty Images
Typesetter: Valerie Levy, Drawing Board Studios
Manufacturing: Steve Bernier

Printed in the United States of America on acid-free paper
19 18 17 16 15 EBM 1 2 3 4 5

For my children,
Rhiannon and Jack Reilly,
for the joy that you bring me,
and for always reminding me
that engagement is
what matters most.

Contents

Acknowledgments

It has been said that it "takes a village" to raise a child, and the same can be said for writing a book. Therefore, I want to express my gratitude for my village.

First and foremost, I want to thank the thousands of students with whom I have worked over the years, who have both inspired me and made this book possible. I truly believe that our students are our greatest teachers, and I thank you all for the wisdom you have brought to my practice. The students who are nearest and dearest to my teaching—the students from the Seven Dwarfs Day Nursery, Chestnut Ridge, New York; Strawtown Elementary School in West Nyack, New York; and the Smith School in Tenafly, New Jersey—have impacted and informed my teaching and my work in profound ways, and to these students and their families, I am forever thankful.

To the students and teachers in the many classrooms I have worked in throughout the years as a consultant and literacy coach, thank you for your welcoming arms, your thoughtful collaboration, and your willingness to go with me on a journey of learning. In particular, I want to express my deepest gratitude to all of my client communities, both past and present, with a special thank you to the Camden Street School in Newark, New Jersey, and in particular to administrators Sam Garrison, Meredith Foote, and Telaya Parham, and teachers Jen Cohan, Liz Masi, and Azan Waddell—I so admire you for all that you do for your students and for creating a beautiful and warm learning community. Thanks to the entire staff, faculty, students, and administration in the Emerson Public Schools in Emerson, New Jersey, but in particular to Jessica Espinoza for your steadfast support of students, teachers, and learning and for your ability to create exemplary learning environments; thanks also to the entire Dwight-Englewood School community and in particular to Michele Sussman, Cecily Gottling, and Mary Jean Alleva and to administrator Susan Abramson for your leadership and unwavering support of learning and growth for adults and students. Thanks to the Nyack Public School System, particularly to teachers Brigid McKenna and Steve Tesher—your glorious work with students amazes and inspires me—and to Winsome Gregory for your vision, leadership, and thoughtfulness; to Cortney Steffens, educator extraordinaire, for opening your classroom to me and for creating a place where students can learn and thrive; to the faculty, administration, and students of the Saddle River Day School for our inspiring collaboration, and your dedicated belief that choice, independence, creativity, and connectedness truly matter; to Liz Veneziano, thank you for the thoughtful and innovative ways that you develop leadership and learning, and for our many collaborations over the years; and to Jean DeSimone, Dana Danziger, Anna Reduce, and Kimberly Marck for allowing me to highlight the wonderful work of your teaching and learning.

To Shirley McPhillips, my former literacy coach and mentor, thank you for knowing my practice and for helping me to grow.

To my former colleagues at the Teacher's College Reading and Writing Project, thank you for providing me with a place where adult learning is valued and can flourish. To Lucy Calkins, thank you for mentoring me and for inspiring me to think big.

For over a decade, I have led a team of amazing educators at LitLife, a professional development organization whose mission is to partner with schools in collaborative and responsive ways. My deepest gratitude to my partners in this endeavor, Jim and Pam Allyn. Thank you for your support and for the belief that children come first. I thank each and every one of my LitLife colleagues, past and present, for the thoughtful and beautiful work that you do and for inspiring me with your humor, wisdom, and grace. To Lindsay Agar, thank you for keeping me organized and supported always, but most especially for your support in this project. Special thanks to Laurie Pastore, Rebecca Bascio, Alisa Kadus, Delia Coppola, and Andrea Lowenkopf for our many conversations and for always pushing my thinking.

To my own professional posse: Bev Gallagher, Ella Urdang, Jaime Margolies, and Sally Rubin-Richards, thank you, thank you, thank you. Words cannot express the gratitude that I have for our collaborations together. Each in your own way has inspired me, mentored me, kept me sane, and reminded me of what matters most in teaching and learning and life.

To my team at Heinemann: thank you for this amazing opportunity to be part of the Heinemann family and for believing that engaging every learner matters so, so much. I thank Alan Huisman for his careful eye to the craft of writing and Monica Crigler for her careful eye on the visual elements of this book. Thanks to Kiele Raymond and Hilary Goff for your work in bringing this book to the final leg and to Kim Cahill for helping to bring this book into the lives of teachers. Most especially, to my editor, Holly Kim Price, words cannot express how happy I am to be working with you again and how thankful I am to you for the joy, support, advice, and wisdom you have given me throughout this process.

To all those listed above, I will pass along a line of gratitude that was recently sent to me by a colleague who was retiring—your voice inside my head has made me better!

My utmost gratitude to the educators who have so positively impacted my own children and their learning; I am thankful to each and every one of you. Special thanks to Patricia Sessa, Rita Algieri, and Jillian Simons for believing in Rhiannon and pushing her to grow, and to Liz Praschil and Damion Logan (Apex Wresting School) for recognizing the light inside of Jack and helping him to succeed and to flourish. I am truly indebted to each of you.

I am so grateful to my family and friends for the ways that they have supported me so that this book could become a reality. To my siblings—Mari, Vicki, Chuck, Danny, Tommy, Pete, Janine, and Christina—thank you for your love and laughter and for memories that I so cherish. To my in-laws, Mary and Jack Reilly, thank you for the love you give to my children and for your belief in faith and family. To my father, Charles Joseph Vitale Sr., for your belief in me and for the voice you have given me that, even though you are gone, continues to live inside of me each and every day. For my parents, John and Pat Hoy, thank you for all that you do for my children, for your encouragement in every aspect of my life, and your love, always. I am who I am because of all of you.

For my many friends, near and far, who have given me joy and love outside of work, I thank you. Special thanks to Marybeth O'Connor, for our lunchtime chats, your sound advice, your love and friendship, always; and to Elena Skinner, for answers to all my visual questions, our many times of laughter, and for loving my children as if they were your own.

And most, most especially, for this family I have created, Kevin, Rhiannon, and Jack Reilly. Rhiannon, you are the daughter that every mother dreams of. You are thoughtful, and kind, and hardworking, and I am inspired by your confidence and your willingness to take what life throws your way. Jack, you are my love and joy, and I am so inspired by your goals and dreams and how you never give up, and by the laughter that you bring to our family and to the world. Kevin, I thank you for your belief in me and support of me that is beyond what I could have ever asked or hoped for; it is because of you that this book is here. I thank you for "making the dough-nuts," and driving to school, and coaching our children, but most of all for your love and friendship, and for being with me on this journey.

Introduction

It is independent reading time and I sit down beside Kaitlyn. We are meeting in a quiet corner of her first-grade classroom in Newark, New Jersey. As a staff developer for Kaitlyn's school, I have been working with Kaitlyn and her peers for the past ten months. Late on a Friday afternoon, we are working together as the other students read independently. Kaitlyn is on her third book.

Glancing over my shoulder, I see that the classroom teacher is transitioning to math. Because it is later in the day, teacher Liz Masi is using a song and one-minute game of freeze dance to transition her students and keep them engaged.

Kaitlyn notices, too, and I say, "Why don't you go dance for a minute and then we'll continue reading?"

Kaitlyn, with all the seriousness a six-year-old can muster, replies, "I don't want to freeze dance, I want to keep reading."

Kaitlyn is engaged in her work, and that is no small task. Kaitlyn is only six years old: there is no sticker, no toy or prize, not even extra fuzzy pom-pom balls in her good behavior jar as a reward for reading and spending time with me. Sure, she wants to read better and reach new milestones; however, this is not what is driving her. Kaitlyn is in what's known as *flow*.

Named by psychology professor Mihaly Csikszentmihalyi (1998), *flow* is the state of optimal focus and immersion in learning. Flow is achieved when students are completely engaged in a task or activity, both cognitively and emotionally.

WHY ENGAGED STUDENT LEARNING IS SO IMPORTANT

Engagement is the act of being invested in learning. Engaged learners are passionate, hardy, persistent, thoughtful, committed, and connected to their work.

In an article titled "Promoting Student Engagement in the Classroom," Bundick and colleagues (2014) specify three "highly interrelated but conceptually distinct" dimensions of engagement:

> *Behavioral engagement* refers to the various learning and academic-oriented behaviors, actions, and involvements in which students engage in school. Examples of behavioral engagement include

Behavioral engagement includes participation, focus, and following school procedures.

participation in school-related activities, attending and contributing to classes, compliance with school rules, and completing assignments, as well as effort put into studying and concentrating on academic tasks. [*Pared down: participation, effort, willingness to be a part of a school community*]

Cognitive engagement involves a psychological investment in learning and mastery of academic material; desire for challenge; enacting metacognitive strategies such as planning, monitoring, and evaluating one's thinking; and self-regulation. [*Pared down: being intent on and active in academic tasks and being willing to challenge oneself and reflect*]

Cognitive engagement is being minds-on in academic tasks and includes willingness to challenge oneself and be reflective.

Emotional engagement refers to students' feelings about their relationships with others in the school environment (e.g., teachers, peers) and the general sense of belonging in the school context that is often derived from such relationships. Additionally, emotional engagement involves students' sense of connectedness to and interest in the academic content, which can be accompanied by a sense of efficacy and confidence regarding their academic ability. [*Pared down: being active and connected with others in the school community and having a strong sense of self*]

Emotional engagement is the "relationship" part of learning and includes interest in learning, connecting with others, and having a strong sense of self.

Kaitlyn exhibits all three dimensions—behavioral engagement, through her effort and ability to stay focused on the task; cognitive engagement, through her self-regulation and desire for challenge; and emotional engagement, through her positive feelings toward our work together.

In *Taking Action on Adolescent Literacy*, Irvin, Meltzer, and Dukes (2007) write:

> Engagement with learning is essential, because it is engagement that leads to sustained interaction and practice. Coaching, instruction, and feedback become critical to ensure that students develop good habits and increase their proficiency. Increased competence typically leads to motivation to engage further, generating a cycle of engagement and developing competence that supports improved student achievement. (30)

As teachers, we want all our students to experience this cycle. Every year we hope for a room filled with Kaitlyns. Regardless of age, grade level, geographic location, type of school, discipline, or curriculum, a student needs to be engaged in his or her learning to excel and succeed.

This book stands on the pillar of this belief.

This is my twenty-fifth year as an educator, and I have come to believe that what we want most for our students—that they be confident, connected, thoughtful, and successful—comes about as the result of their engagement in learning. Our students are relying on us to create classrooms in which this engagement can happen.

Engagement may begin with the motivation to engage further, but true engagement is all-encompassing. Motivation expert Paul Marciano (2012) compares techniques for motivating adults to windup toys, which wind down and need to be wound up again. The same is true of students in relation to learning. If motivating them to learn merely involves winding them up—providing the prize—their engagement will be short lived. Engagement is both self-sustaining and long term. It lives and breathes within students and keeps them going for the long haul.

In an article in *Gallup Business Journal* titled "Not Enough Students Are Success-Ready," Shane Lopez (2014) shares some results of the spring 2013 Gallup poll that pertain to student engagement:

> While 54% of students surveyed in the U.S. are hopeful, almost half lack hope for the future, reporting they feel stuck in their lives (32%) or discouraged about the future (14%). Hopeful students take their education more seriously and bring positive ideas and energy to the learning process, making emotional engagement in school more likely. A similar percentage of students are engaged with school (55%). But almost half are either not engaged (28%) or are actively disengaged (17%). Students' emotional engagement with school is the non-cognitive measure most directly related to academic achievement.

Even students themselves understand how much engagement matters to their learning.

HOW WE DEVELOP STUDENT ENGAGEMENT

Engagement is cultivated, not taught. In this book I identify and show how to apply classroom components—strategies, tools, and principles of teaching—that cultivate and develop student engagement.

Chapter 1 examines the classroom learning environment and the role it plays in student engagement. This environment begins with the physical space but goes beyond it to include emotional and cognitive space. When we establish the physical, emotional, and cognitive space of a classroom, a year of engagement can begin.

The next step is starting the school year on the right foot, which is addressed in Chapter 2. The first few weeks set the path for engagement. In both teaching and life, there is no place to begin but at the beginning.

Chapter 3 deals with assessment. Students' learning and their level of engagement, as a community but also individually, need to be accurately measured throughout the school year.

Chapter 4 examines instructional strategies and tools that elicit a high level of student engagement. Grounded in the gradual-release-of-responsibility approach to instruction (Pearson and Gallagher 1983), this chapter provides strategies for engaging students during whole-class lessons, in small-group instruction, and during one-to-one teaching.

Chapter 5 examines the seminal principle of choice—why choice is important and how to implement it during a year of teaching and learning.

Chapter 6 looks at tools for engagement in the context of popular culture and the larger learning community. It discusses ways to use popular culture and technology to engage students and presents examples of how to enlist the larger community (families, local nonprofit organizations and businesses, a school's faculty and staff) in efforts to build and sustain student engagement.

The appendix is a blueprint for putting it all together. It reveals the scope of these principles, strategies, and tools and suggests a sequence for implementing them during a school year.

Teaching is an amazing and unique profession. We can continually widen and develop our awareness of what works best for our students. Think of your Kaitlyns. What will it take to make every student a Kaitlyn? This book will help you move forward on the path to cultivating student engagement for all learners!

Chapter

One

Cultivating Engagement
Through the Environment

My first teaching experience was in an early childhood center that was originally part of a Waldorf school. I was struck by how different the classrooms looked in this learning community! According to the Waldorf philosophy, classrooms should contain a warm, inviting, and homelike environment. In fact, classrooms are built from the ground up. Consideration is given to the color of the walls, the lighting in the room, and accessibility to the outdoors. Classrooms for younger children are painted in warm hues. For students in grades 4 and above, who are able to think abstractly, classrooms are painted in cool colors. In his book about the Waldorf philosophy, *Understanding Waldorf Education: Teaching from the Inside Out*, Jack Petrash (2002) explains:

> Rudolf Steiner designed Waldorf Education around the simple idea that children have within them three fundamental forces impelling them toward physical, emotional, and mental activity. As a teacher I have always appreciated that these three capacities were called *forces*. This reminded me continually that if I did not recognize my students' need to be engaged in these three ways, these three significant tendencies would *force* themselves on my attention in less appropriate ways. (24)

These physical, emotional, and mental forces influence not only the types of activities in which students engage but also the classroom environment.

A few years later, I was introduced to the Reggio Emilia (a town in Northern Italy) approach to learning. The physical environment incorporates a tremendous amount of student work as well as relevant objects found by students, and the various spaces in the classroom (I call them nooks) are arranged to promote engagement and provide ample opportunity for small- and large-group learning. In fact, the room is considered an "additional teacher." In a post on the classroom environment from *A Classroom Full of Curiosity and Wonder*, bloggers Thall and Shawana (2012) quote educator Loris Malaguzzi:"We place enormous value on the role of the environment as a motivating and animating force in creating spaces for relations, options, and emotional and cognitive situations that produce a sense of well-being and security."

We learn from these two philosophies that classroom environments need to be warm, inviting, and homelike; include student work and objects that resonate with students; promote active, thoughtful learning; and most importantly, be physically arranged in a way that permits learning and collaborating in various student groupings.

THE PHYSICAL CLASSROOM ENVIRONMENT

The physical classroom space includes the floors, walls, and furniture; storage facilities; and student materials. Educator Eric Jensen's work on brain research and the connection between the brain, the classroom environment, and successful learning has influenced how classrooms are physically arranged. In his book *Teaching with the Brain in Mind* (2005), he states:

> From an observer's perspective, engagement is a simple, easily understood concept. It means that, as learners, we "bring more to the table." We focus our sight, pitch our ears, and physically attend to the process at hand. All teachers know that engaged students are usually happier than disconnected ones who have isolated tasks to do. (35)

He lists five variables to consider in the physical space of a room—seating, temperature, lighting, noise, and building design (82)—and identifies seven elements architectural firms consider when designing a school:

- acoustics
- daytime lighting
- ecology
- temperature, humidity, and ventilation
- learning spaces
- optimal views

- school size
- staff areas.

It would be wonderful if every student could learn in a new, up-to-date building possessing all these features, but that's not always possible. However, we as teachers do control many aspects of a classroom's physical environment. Considering these components has a profound impact on student engagement.

Arrange Classroom Furniture

The placement of desks and other classroom furniture should encourage active learning. Desks should be arranged in flexible clusters or pods so students can easily collaborate with peers and participate in small-group instruction. There should be ample space between these clusters so that students can move freely from one area of the room to another.

For example, although she was thoughtful about room arrangement, teacher Liz Masi struggled with how to arrange the desks in her first-grade inclusion classroom with twenty-six students. The room was relatively small, and the desks had been handed down from classrooms at various grade levels and were therefore of different sizes. At first, she placed them in pairs to provide a sense of order and discourage off-task behavior. However, this arrangement took up a lot of space, made it difficult to move from one area of the classroom to another, and did not lend itself to collaborations larger than pairs. In addition, all students faced the front of the room all the time; those in back were far away from her, the anchor charts, and the word wall. She therefore decided to cluster the desks into six pods (four or five desks each) around a carpet facing the interactive whiteboard (see Figures 1.1a and 1.1b).

Figures 1.1a and 1.1b Photos of Elementary and Secondary Model Classrooms

The backs of the chairs, where the students store their materials, are easily accessible throughout the day. Desks within the pods face different directions for varied reasons. Students face each other when collaborating during a lesson or activity, but individual students can face various sides of the classroom, depending on what works best for them. For example, Giovanni's attention tends to drift during lessons. Proximity to Liz and the visual aids is extremely important. Therefore, he always sits in pod 1, 2, or 3, in a desk facing the front of the classroom, so he can see the interactive whiteboard. Messiah's desk, on the other hand, is in the pod closest to the classroom closet and faces that wall. During lessons, he can shift either his body or his chair to face front, but during independent or group work, it is important that he not be distracted. Carla, who has an individualized education program (IEP), always sits in a pod toward the back of the classroom, close to the two small-group instruction tables, which Liz's colleague and collaborative teacher, Yasmin, use when a lesson needs to be modified for Carla and other students.

Student engagement is cultivated when placement of furniture considers flow, direction, proximity to teachers, and materials.

Manage Materials

Students, not just the teacher, need to be responsible for using and storing materials. When students care about their physical environment and own every aspect of their classroom, they are engaged in learning.

Gayle, a former colleague who taught third grade, waited to arrange the storage areas of her classroom until after the students arrived. On the first day of school, students found a large box in the classroom library. In it were most of the materials that belonged in the library. During the first few days of school, her students would decide how the books would be organized, create labels for book bins, devise checklists for borrowing and returning materials, and arrange the materials. This level of ownership assures enthusiastic and thoughtful use of the classroom library, not just in September but throughout the year.

A common (and valid) complaint I hear from teachers is that students don't manage their materials well. Students are less likely to lose items when they know where they go and care that they get there! At the beginning of the year, Liz introduces a filing system for anecdotal notes and center work. Folders are personalized by the students and easily accessible by Liz, Yasmin, and the students. Index cards with site words, center materials, notebooks, book bins, and other storage devices are also personalized and stored, in a way the makes sense to students, in an easily accessible area.

The idea here is not that teachers compete for a good housekeeping award but rather create classrooms that are meaningful to students and free of clutter. Researchers at the Princeton University Neuroscience Institute have found that clutter prevents a learner from maintaining focus and engagement (Doland 2011).

Use Wall Space

My experience in the Waldorf school, my exploration of the Reggio Emilia philosophy, and the work of Eric Jensen have all shown me how important wall space is to student engagement. Many elementary school teachers think classrooms should be bright and colorful places—the brighter and more colorful, the better the learning and engagement. Anchor charts, premade posters, schedules, word walls, student work, and so on adorn the walls. Conversely, at the secondary level, there is typically nothing on the walls. Each scenario is an extreme. The key to student engagement is to use the wall space to create community, capture learning, manage the class, and display resources.

Think first about the colors used in the room. Eric Jensen (2005) suggests that the walls be a warm, muted color and that the print displayed be visually appealing but not visually overstimulating.

Next, consider the amount of print. Provide important information (a daily schedule or the lesson objective), but remember that less is more: don't use more words than students need. Also, rethink how you display daily learning. Create anchor charts of learning but think of most class charts as temporary. Not all charts need to be on display all the time. Anchor charts are important; they connect the learners to the learning (see Figure 1.2a and 1.2b). However, the more

Figure 1.2a and 1.2b Elementary and Secondary Examples of Charts—Print and Digital

charts you have, the less your students engage with them. They become wallpaper, no longer serving the purpose intended.

The 4Teachers website (www.4Teachers.org) has a "classroom architect" tool that lets you virtually experiment with the physical environment of your classroom by dropping and dragging desks, storage units, technology equipment, and other elements of physical space (see Figure 1.3). This experimentation is done without the heavy lifting of actually moving classroom furniture around and works with the exact physical dimensions of a classroom. When planning and arranging your physical environment, you can also use the checklist in Figure 1.4.

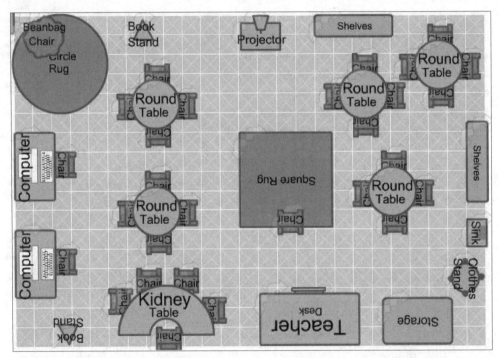

Figure 1.3 Classroom Architect in Action

THE EMOTIONAL CLASSROOM ENVIRONMENT

Think back to your own experiences as a student and recall a classroom that you loved and where you felt successful. Conversely, think of a class or learning experience that you did not enjoy, one where you felt unsuccessful. If you examine the conditions of each of those experiences, some of what led you to be successful, or led to your perceived lack of success, can be tied to the emotional environment.

✓	**Desk Arrangement**	Desks are arranged in "pods" so students can engage in both whole-class and small-group learning. Desk placement allows you and classroom materials to be close to your students.
✓	**Additional Seating or Nooks**	Additional seating and learning spaces (including tables if possible) are flexible and easily accessible.
✓	**Technology**	The technology area is accessible during whole-group and small-group activities.
✓	**Materials**	Materials storage is organized, personalized, and accessible.
✓	**Wall Space**	Materials displayed on the walls support learning, they don't detract from it; they engage students but do not overwhelm them with everything you want them to know or have taught them.

Figure 1.4 Physical Classroom Environment Checklist

The emotional environment encompasses the "relationship" part of the classroom—tone, rituals, and student self-efficacy. Eric Jensen (2008) discusses the learning principles leading to high engagement. The principle of emotional–physical state dependency reveals why the emotional environment is so important:

> Learning occurs through a complex set of continuous signals, which inform your brain about whether to form a memory, or not. Both emotional and bodily states influence our attention, memory, learning, meaning, and behavior through these signaling systems. (21)

Engagement increases when students are emotionally connected.

Kristy Cooper (2014) claims that student engagement is directly correlated to success in high school and that some teachers are much more successful at engaging students than others. She defines emotional engagement as "the extent to which a student enjoys a class, feels comfortable and interested, and wants to do well." If we want students to be emotionally engaged, we need to consider the emotional environment of a classroom.

Based on my work in classrooms, there are three ways to create a positive and engaging emotional environment: classroom tone, classroom rituals, and student self-efficacy.

Develop Classroom Tone

The tone of a classroom is amorphous and hard to pinpoint. After all, how do we incorporate or develop something that we cannot literally hold in our hands? *Tone* is not only the tone of voice used by those who speak but also the feeling one gets while being present. This feeling, or tone, is encouraged and cultivated through the interactions of members of the classroom community.

Balance Classroom Voices

The first step is to create a balance of voices between teacher and student and student and student. Classrooms where students are emotionally engaged are classrooms that respect and value student voices. One of the best pieces of advice I received from a staff developer was to remember that my voice is not the only one that matters. Think carefully each day about the amount of space your voice takes up in comparison to the voices of your students.

One way I balance student voices is by asking my students to say back to me what I've just said. By asking them to clarify or restate what they are learning ("Who can say back to me what we have just explored in our lesson today?"), I am putting forth their voices and checking their understanding of my teaching. I also say back to my students what they've just said to me, modeling how to listen and clarify ("So if I heard you correctly, you explained that . . .").

I also ask students to interact with one another: "Turn to the student next to you and discuss the way you will solve this math problem." "Turn and discuss what Jasmine just explained to us. Do you agree or disagree?" Brain research indicates that adult learners do not have the capacity to listen for more than twenty minutes at a time. For students, who are still cultivating this capacity, the amount of time is less. They need to interact during a lesson.

In a classroom with an imbalance between teacher and peer voices, engagement will be low. Think critically about how much space each voice takes up in the room (including your own!) and create a meaningful balance.

Vary Noise Level

There should be a variety of noise levels in a classroom, depending on age level and type of instruction. Noise is potentially a sign of excitement, interaction, and engagement. Many classrooms feel too noisy; in some, the only noise is the voice of the teacher. Here's a good rule of thumb:

Class Component	Noise Level (on a scale of 0–5)
Whole-class teaching	1–2
Independent practice	0–1
Collaborative practice	2–3

The noise level, as a general rule, should never exceed level 3

Encourage Risk Taking

Taking risks is an essential component of engagement; students need to feel they can be active, participate, think aloud, and grow ideas together. If the classroom culture is such that students are always intent on getting the "right answer," their participation decreases. Students who do not feel comfortable sharing information for fear of being wrong will silently disconnect. Honoring participation and encouraging risk taking sends a powerful message to students about what is valued in the classroom and cultivates both a positive emotional environment and student willingness to be engaged and active at all times.

Use Positive Nonverbal Communication

Individuals communicate through nonverbal mannerisms and expressions that deeply impact the emotional tone of a classroom. Keeping these interactions positive keeps the emotional engagement high. This doesn't mean we can't provide authentic feedback, even express disappointment or disapproval; it does mean that we need to remain keenly aware of what our body says that our voices do not. Here are five ways to strengthen the emotional environment nonverbally:

1. *Smile regularly.* As Orphan Annie so wisely sings in the musical based on the iconic comic strip, you're never fully dressed without a smile. Smiling creates a warm, inviting environment and encourages positive interactions. Classrooms should be joyous places for learning. Communicate this joy by smiling.

2. *Stay close to your students* (see Figure 1.5). Proximity is important—where you sit or stand when presenting a lesson, how you position yourself when you are working with a small group, how you lean in during one-to-one interactions.

Figure 1.5 An Example of Teacher–Student Proximity

3. *Listen actively.* Students need to feel you're genuinely listening. Demonstrating a listening stance—facing the speaker, nodding your head, pausing—not only engages students but also models how to listen to others.

4. *Signify positive and authentic reinforcement and feedback.* Give a thumbs up, nod, silently applaud.

5. *Suggest nonverbal ways students can communicate with one another* (see Figure 1.6). Nonverbal signals keep students engaged and create a positive but rigorous classroom tone. They also help keep the noise level to a hum. In Jen Cohan's third-grade class, nonverbal signals keep the communication and engagement high.

Establish Classroom Rituals

Rituals, big and small, connect and engage communities. Here are just a few that consistently build the emotional environment in classrooms at any level:

- *Daily and yearly greetings.* As a classroom teacher, I greeted my students on the first day of school with a handshake. (Most students, whether in elementary, middle, or high school, are not used to shaking hands with an adult. Their reactions ranged from shock to delight.) On the last day of school, I sent them off on their next adventure with another handshake. This ritual can set the tone for the year. You should also greet students every day. I try to say hello to each student if not daily, then at least a few times a week. A direct, specific "Good morning" or "How are you?" goes a long way. A high five ends the day on a positive, celebratory note.

- *Rituals around words.* My favorite classroom ritual, one I have used with every class from preschool to grad school, is to begin each day with the words of others. I read aloud at the beginning of each day, period, or class. It has a profound emotional impact.

- *Positive affirmations.* Positive acknowledgments (frequently missing in secondary classrooms) come in many forms and can be given at any time.

They can be posted on a bulletin board or delivered orally. Middle school students love the weekly "shout-outs" in which I give credit to a few students for accomplishment, improvement, or generosity to others in our community.

Reinforce Student Self-Efficacy

Self-efficacy is the belief students have about themselves and their capacities and is another component that builds a positive emotional environment. Psychologist Albert Bandura (1997) states, "Perceived self-efficacy is defined as people's beliefs about their capabilities to produce designated levels of performance that exercise influence over events that affect their lives. Self-efficacy beliefs determine how people feel, think, motivate themselves, and behave" (2).

Self-efficacy is developed over the course of a lifetime, beginning at home. As teachers, we have the profound ability to both develop and positively impact students' self-efficacy and therefore their level of engagement. Research shows that students with high self-efficacy persevere, are more likely to accomplish short-term tasks and long-term goals, and experience overall greater success in school.

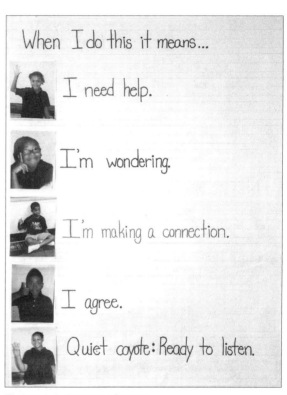

Figure 1.6 Nonverbal Symbols

Conversely, students with low self-efficacy have low aspirations, have difficulty completing tasks in school, and are disengaged overall.

Howard Margolis and Patrick McCabe (2006) outline four sources of self-efficacy: enactive mastery, vicarious experiences, verbal persuasion, and physiological reaction.

> Self-efficacy is what students infer from the information from these sources; it is the judgment they make about their ability to succeed on a specific task or set of related tasks. By understanding and systematically using these sources, teachers can influence struggling learners' self-efficacy.

Figure 1.7 Picture of Original Student Success System

A combination of those four sources works best, but I am particularly concerned with physiological reactions. Here's an example.

During an individual reading session with me, Darnell (one of Liz's first graders) was having a particularly hard time with a text. The text was a simple narrative at his instructional level, with few unfamiliar features or complexities. At one point one of the characters, Kate, goes to a ranch; Darnell lives in a city in New Jersey and had no frame of reference for this. That said, the text was much more challenging for Darnell than I anticipated. After some probing, I discovered that he was distracted by his concern that his car was not going to move up on the levels chart. Liz had created a system for acknowledging students' success—a board on which cars representing the students moved up level by level as their reading ability improved during the year (see Figure 1.7)—and Darnell was preoccupied with how far and how fast his car was, or wasn't, moving.

Liz and I talked about this method of giving positive affirmations. There are a number of good points. This success system is a growth model. Each learner's achievement is recognized, and the goal is not to achieve a score (or have that score correlate to their reading level) but to show improvement. Also, the symbol of the car is developmentally appropriate for first grade and a great metaphor—these students are going places!

We then discussed how it could be improved so it wouldn't negatively impact Darnell's self-efficacy. First, the chart would represent growth nonnumerically. Rather than going from level 1 to 2 to 3 and so on, the students would move from the starting line to the first corner, then on to the next lap, and so on. In addition, the advancement of the students could be captured in a variety of ways and perhaps even use a different symbol (she ultimately decided to use bees moving from flower to flower) and would be triggered by a variety of growth factors: engagement and effort, completion of work, ability to stay on task, and achievement. See Figure 1.8.

Figure 1.8 New Student Success System

THE COGNITIVE CLASSROOM ENVIRONMENT

The cognitive environment is the academic tone of a learning community—the rigor and expectations in the classroom. Kristy Cooper (2014) defines cognitive engagement as the mind work students apply to learning—the "extent to which a student applies mental energy, thinks about the content, tries to figure out new material, and grapples with mental challenges" (365). Matthew Bundick and his colleagues (2014) define it this way: "Cognitive engagement involves a psychological investment in learning and mastery of academic material; desire for challenge; enacting metacognitive strategies such as planning, monitoring, and evaluating one's thinking; and self-regulation" (3). Cognitive engagement and the creation of a cognitive environment are essential to student academic success. We want students to invest in and plan their learning and challenge themselves.

The cognitive environment in Azan Waddell's seventh-grade classroom is well developed. His students are consistently clear on what is expected of them. Azan works thoughtfully to create an academically rigorous environment by considering the cognitive aspects. This is achieved through a four-pronged approach.

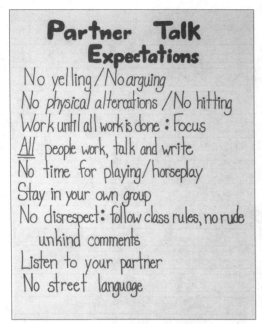

Figure 1.9 Partner Expectations Chart

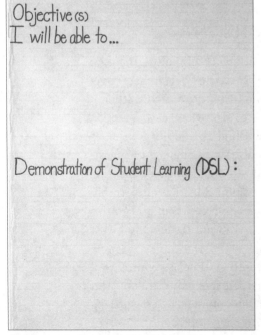

Figure 1.10 Classroom Chart for "I Will" Statements

Set High Expectations and Communicate Them Orally and in Writing

High expectations have a profound effect on student efficacy, effort, engagement, and achievement. Set high personal and community expectations for class work, personal conduct, participation, and quantity and quality of work, and don't lower these expectations for struggling students. Instead, outline a clear trajectory of teaching that will enable every student to reach these high expectations. Then communicate these high expectations orally and in writing. Purposeful and specific checklists and anchor charts, on chart paper or an interactive whiteboard, prompt students to meet the expectations independently. Display anchor charts where students can see them, keep them up throughout the year, and refer to them often. (Figure 1.9 is an example of an anchor chart.)

Anchor charts capture verbal directions and provide students with tangible and clear directions. In fact, in my own classroom, I would frequently refer to anchor charts, verbally or through a nonverbal signal, to remind students of expectations and procedures. In fact, students in Azan's class do the same thing. They will frequently be found pointing to, referring to, or even standing near and referencing the partner expectations chart when working through difficulty in collaborative learning situations.

Establish Consequences

There is nothing punitive or harsh about Azan's classroom, but there are appropriate consequences for not handing in assignments or misbehavior. Students are encouraged to see the consequence as an opportunity to take a better course of action and are positively acknowledged for improved work and behavior. The entire school community works hard to guarantee that there are fair, nonpunitive, appropriate consequences in place.

Communicating expectations in writing ensures that expectations are clear and that students are cognitively engaged.

Make Learning an Active Process

Make the learning explicit, make the learning meaningful, and then monitor and measure that learning. Students need to "do" as they are learning.

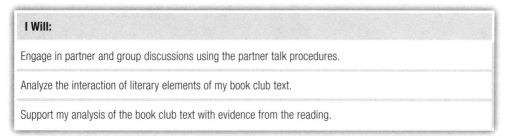

I Will:

Engage in partner and group discussions using the partner talk procedures.

Analyze the interaction of literary elements of my book club text.

Support my analysis of the book club text with evidence from the reading.

Figure 1.11 Sample "I Will" Statements

In Azan's classroom, student learning begins with objectives phrased as "I will" statements (see Figure 1.10). These statements are sometimes created for students and reviewed at the beginning of the learning. More often, these statements are created with the students' participation; they need to take an active part in planning and implementing their learning (see Figure 1.11).

The learning then continues through lessons designed to bring about full student participation; these lessons include direct instruction, students' attempts to apply that instruction, any necessary clarification, and differentiated independent practice that reflects the high expectations and rigorous cognitive tone of the classroom. (The lesson format is discussed more fully in Chapter 4.) Figure 1.12 is an example of a schedule for

Figure 1.12 Independent Work and Small-Group Schedule

Day/Period	Must Do	Can Do	Comments/Reflection
Monday			
Tuesday			
Wednesday			
Thursday			
Friday			

Figure 1.13 Checklist for Independent Learning

independent and small-group work. To promote active learning and thus high cognitive engagement, many teachers also use a weekly independent learning checklist to help students manage their learning. One such weekly checklist would include both what students must do in a week and what they can do as part of their independent learning and practice; see the example in Figure 1.13.

Cultivate Creativity

Creativity enables students to be active, thoughtful, divergent, and engaged. Many fear that creativity has been on the decline in schools for the last decade. In a *Newsweek* article from June 2010, the authors Po Bronson and Ashley Merryman explore the creativity crisis in America and the decline of creativity in all students, but most especially in students in grades kindergarten through grade 6. Bronson and Merryman (2010) state:

> [Creativity] is not just about sustaining our nation's economic growth. All around us are matters of national and international importance that are crying out for creative solutions, from saving the Gulf of Mexico to bringing peace to Afghanistan to delivering health care. Such solutions emerge from a healthy marketplace of ideas, sustained by a populous constantly contributing original ideas and receptive to the ideas of others. (45)

To be creative, one must use divergent thinking (generate many unique, out-of-the box ideas) and then convergent thinking (bring those ideas together in a creation or solution). Our schools need to be places where students have time for exploration and teachers facilitate and nourish creative thinking. Creativity is essential to the mindfulness required in a cognitive environment. It needs to be both valued and cultivated.

In Michele Sussman's third-grade classroom, creativity is an integral part of the daily work. Michele and her colleagues Cecily Gottling and Susan Abramson honor student creativity by providing ways for students to use divergent thinking, explore options, and produce something original. For example, see the literacy and math exercises in Figures 1.14 and 1.15.

In both instances, students are asked to show everything they know about the word or the number. There is both a "right" answer and a way for students to think outside the box, express themselves in a variety of ways, and demonstrate a deep understanding of related concepts. Both exercises come at the end of a lot of focused instruction and require students to use the competencies they have developed during the unit. Standing on the shoulders of the belief that when students are exposed to, explicitly taught, and given opportunities for independent practice with feedback, they become both playful and accurate and thus creative.

These components enable students to take an active role in their learning and practice, and therefore create a cognitive tone that cultivates engagement. When teachers pay attention to the cognitive environment, then student achievement is positively impacted.

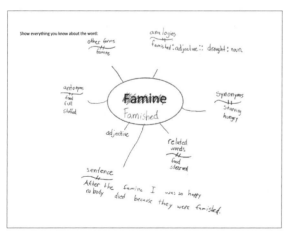

Figure 1.14 Exploring Vocabulary Through Many Lenses

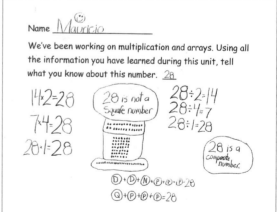

Figure 1.15 Exploring Whole Numbers in Divergent and Creative Ways

■ ENVIRONMENT CHECKLIST

The Physical Classroom Environment

☐ Arrange Classroom Furniture

    ☐ Is your classroom organized in a way that allows for flow, collaboration, and active learning?

☐ Manage Materials

    ☐ Are your materials stored in an easily organized and accessible way?

☐ Use Wall Space

    ☐ Are your walls painted a color that will engage yet not distract students?

    ☐ Are anchor charts and decorations accessible to learners but not visually overstimulating?

The Emotional Classroom Environment

☐ Develop Classroom Tone

    ☐ Are voices balanced between teacher and student and student and student?

    ☐ Is the noise level in the room conducive to learning?

    ☐ Is risk taking valued and cultivated in all learners?

    ☐ Is there a system for nonverbal communication in collaborative settings?

☐ Establish Classroom Rituals

    ☐ Are there classroom rituals, such as daily greetings or weekly meetings, that build the emotional environment?

    ☐ Are positive affirmations used to acknowledge students?

☐ Reinforce Student Self-Efficacy

    Is there a system to acknowledge growth and celebrate successes?

The Cognitive Classroom Environment

☐ Set High Expectations and Communicate Them Orally and in Writing

    ☐ Are there high expectations for each learner?

    ☐ Are expectations communicated in anchor charts?

    ☐ Are expectations communicated in student checklists?

☐ Establish Consequences

    ☐ Are consequences fair, explicit, and used appropriately?

☐ Make Learning an Active Process

    ☐ Are daily learning statements—"I will" statements—used to clarify and guide learning?

    ☐ Do lessons include student involvement?

    ☐ Are checklists used to manage students and keep learning active?

☐ Cultivate Creativity

    ☐ Do students have time to explore?

    ☐ Do you facilitate and nourish creative thinking?

Chapter

Two

Setting the Course to Engage Every Learner

When I was growing up in suburban New York, my eight siblings and I would catch fireflies on early summer nights. There was nothing more satisfying than capturing the brightest and biggest one, first in your hand and then in a jar. It was a ritual that marked the arrival of summer's lazy, carefree hours.

As teachers, we need rituals to set the course for a successful, engaging year for our learners.

Paula Denton and Roxann Kriete (2000) identify four intentions, or broad objectives, for the first six weeks of school: create a climate and tone of warmth and safety; teach the schedule and routines of the school day; introduce the students to the physical environment of the classroom and the school; and establish expectations for learning (3–4). Michigan educator Bill Cecil (2007) refers to the beginning of the year as "setting the table" and suggests that teachers spend two weeks at the beginning of the year establishing a positive, safe learning environment (14–15). During these first few weeks, we need to develop routines for the classroom and establish a community of learners.

Therefore, it is during these first few weeks of school that we set the course for a year of student engagement. During this time, we want to develop routines for the classroom and develop our community of learners.

Developing Classroom Routines

Routines are the glue that binds our day. When I wake in the morning, I take my daily allotment of medicine and vitamins, do a few yoga stretches, check the weather and traffic, and then go down the hall to my home office to check email. If I do not start my day with this routine, the day feels different and I am out of sorts. The same is true for our students. They crave routine to help them make sense of the day and help them feel secure in their environment and ultimately in their learning.

Research supports the positive effect of routines on students and student learning. Linda Shalaway (1998) discusses the work of researcher David Berliner, who claims that teachers are "executives" who make the daily decisions that affect student learning and that we can only do this by managing routines (26). Gaea Leinhardt and her colleagues at the University of Pittsburgh's Learning Research and Development Center have also explored the importance of routines to student learning:

> Successful teachers use the first days of school to establish and rehearse routines which permit instruction to proceed fluidly and efficiently. Routines, shared socially scripted patterns of behavior, serve to reduce the cognitive complexity of the instructional environment. (1987, 135)

Classroom routines can be different in different classrooms, but the three routines essential to student engagement are classroom meetings, student talk, and transitions.

Classroom Meetings

Like any well-run organization, classrooms should have meetings. These meetings set a tone, establish expectations, and provide structure. Classroom meetings can happen at any time of the day or week, but I find a morning meeting and an end-of-week meeting essential.

The morning meeting (see Figure 2.1) can be set up in various ways, from the very structured to the very open and organic. Mine falls somewhere in between and includes three consistent elements: a read-aloud, the daily schedule, and class news.

I began implementing a morning read-aloud based on research reported in *Becoming a Nation of Readers* (Anderson et al. 1985). The researchers found that the single most important factor in developing a reader was whether or not the child was read to. The single most important factor! I knew then that I had to incorporate read-alouds into my daily and weekly schedule in various ways and decided to begin each

Figure 2.1 Picture of Class Meeting

morning meeting with one. I read something different aloud each day—something that I want my students to hear and experience as learners. These are stand-alone pieces, between two and three minutes long, representing a great variety of genres, structures, authors, and purposes. There are many benefits to starting the morning this way, but the best is how quickly the students, whatever their grade level, unite as active learners.

The daily schedule segment is short but essential for establishing the day's tone and expectations. We review the schedule (which is very similar day to day) and highlight any special event, celebration, or change in the daily routine. Students begin the day grounded, knowing what they have to navigate.

The class news portion of the morning meeting is more organic, different every day, but still integral. Some days the announcements pertain to everyone: upcoming events, class accolades, class trips. Other days, the news is personal to a particular student or group of students: a birthday, a bar or bat mitzvah, a win by the soccer team.

I use end-of-week meetings to celebrate accomplishments, address issues of fairness that may be bubbling under the surface (dress code infractions or pulling one's weight in group projects, for example), and encourage students to share their reflections. For five minutes or so, we discuss the week about to end:

Using the routine of a weekly meeting gives students the time and space to celebrate milestones or address concerns.

- What was the best part? The worst?

- Identify one part/moment of the week when you were successful as a learner. Draw, write, and then speak this moment to celebrate!

- Reflect on this week's goals. Did we meet them? If not, why not?

- Set a goal for the upcoming week. These goals can be about organization (managing materials, cubbies, desks, or lockers), a particular discipline (achieving competency in new math or accomplishing work on a science project), or a habit of mind (keeping focused during writing workshop or completing all homework on time).

Student Talk

One of the most effective ways to engage students is by letting them talk. Research shows that teachers talk 80 percent of the time during a lesson or class period, leaving little time for students to talk (and ultimately to engage in learning). In addition to increasing the amount of time students talk and interact, we need to create routines for enabling them to do so. These routines encourage risk taking, personal responsibility, and ongoing student engagement.

The first consideration is *when* students will actively participate. Chiming in at the beginning of a lesson is ineffective: students focus on what they want to say, not what we are teaching. Equally ineffective is asking a student to "hold that thought": learning is disrupted and focus is lost. Students need to know when they are invited and expected to participate.

My approach is, after a brief period of instruction, to invite students to participate by way of a short conversation—to turn and talk (see Figure 2.2):

- I say: "What do we notice about the first three steps of that equation? Turn and talk." Or: "What do you think about what Giselle just shared? Turn and talk about that." Or: "What do you notice about how the author is using the first-person voice in the text? Turn and talk."

- Students move to face their partner(s)—pair, trio, quartet—and make eye contact.

- Students take turns talking while I listen in. (I may establish thirty-second limits to ensure each person gets to share.)

If we also encourage students to share ideas during instruction, we need to establish a way for them to indicate their desire to contribute. Do we want them to raise their hand, give a thumbs up, nod their head? Handing or tossing an object—a stick or a ball—to students who wish to share ideas adds a kinesthetic element.

Figure 2.2 Student Turn and Talk

Third-grade teacher Dana Danziger uses a small, squishy ball to invite and engage student participation. During whole-class lessons, she moves around the room, making eye contact with her learners. A student nods when he or she wants to share. If it's an appropriate time or if Dana has just asked a question, she throws the ball to this learner, who catches it, shares her or his thinking, and, depending on the situation, either tosses it back to Dana or to another student. The kinesthetic element of the routine keeps students engaged.

In addition to considering when and how students will participate, we need to consider all the voices in our classroom, the meek as well as the bold. Considering and managing the balance of voices is essential to creating equity of voices and engagement for all. One year when I was teaching fourth grade, this was a particular challenge. Although I had introduced a routine for talk and it was running smoothly, I struggled to involve all voices. The conversations were uneven and monopolized by a few students. After some discussion and trial and error, the students and I together instituted this routine for whole-class conversations:

- Students each had a certain number of chips; they surrendered one each time they wanted to contribute to a class conversation.

- When they had used all their chips, they could participate by using nonverbal signals to communicate their thinking (see Chapter 1 for more information) or recording their thoughts on sticky notes and placing them on an "additional thoughts" chart.

- Students who had difficulty inserting themselves into conversations could ask a buddy for help. For example, Tomo would look at his best friend, Jonathan, who would announce to the class, "Tomo has something he would like to say." Tomo would then surrender a chip and share his thinking.

This is one scenario that worked with a particular group of students. What is important to note about all of the suggestions listed above is that each is a routine to cultivate and manage student talk. Consider your specific student population and create routines that will encourage risk taking, personal responsibility, and ongoing student engagement.

Transitions

Regardless of the age level or subject you teach, it is important to create routines for transitions between subjects or class periods. Managing transitions is essential to student engagement. Planned transition routines minimize behavior issues and reboot student attention. Robert Marzano and his coauthors (2008) recommend three essential elements:

- establish rules and procedures for recurring situations
- practice transitions and responses to classroom interruptions
- appoint student leaders during transitions and interruptions.

No matter the routine, it should be simple, thoughtful, and fun! Let's look at some examples.

Liz Masi's routine to ensure that her first graders leave the classroom in an orderly way to go to lunch or a special is a simple "One, two, three, four." When Liz says, "One," all students stand; on "two," they push in their chair; on "three," they move their body away from their desk to face the classroom door; on "four," they fall into line as Liz points to one table at a time, starting with the weekly line leader's table. At the primary level, this routine incorporates what Marzano and colleagues recommend and is simple, thoughtful, fun.

Incorporating movement when transitioning from subject to subject (from reading to math, for example) reinvigorates students' attention and their thought processes. William Strean (2011) states: "A great way to increase energy and engagement is with physical movement. It is ideal when movement can be incorporated directly with the learning objectives of the day, but short activities simply to shift attention and awaken the students are beneficial."

Liz's routine for transitioning between subjects is standing and stretching, followed by one-minute segment of freeze dance. Again, this is simple, thoughtful, and fun.

In upper elementary classrooms, transitions can take the form of small breaks. In my fourth-grade classroom, I created a five-minute routine in which students put away materials they had finished using, gathered new materials needed for the next portion of our day, and grabbed a snack. It helped me manage materials and fueled the students' brains and bodies.

Transitions can also involve music. Research reveals that music can humanize, personalize, and energize instruction; tap into students' interests and elicit positive feelings and associations; and involve students in relevant and meaningful interaction (Dunlap and Lowenthal 2010). Many middle and high schools minimize or eliminate bells between classes and instead play music over the central PA system. When the music begins to fade, students know the next period is about to begin. This type of transition is tailored to the secondary learner, yet is also simple, thoughtful, and fun.

> *Regardless of the age* or subject you teach, it is important to create routines for transitions between subjects or periods. Attending to the "in-between" of learning will yield high engagement.

BUILDING COMMUNITY

The first weeks of school are jam-packed with items on our to-do list—giving out all requisite forms, familiarizing students with our classroom routines, and beginning to teach! We want to remember to take the time to build a healthy and vibrant classroom community. In doing so, we not only set the stage for a year of engaged learning, we get to know our students and give them time to get to know one another—and themselves—better as well. Mara Sapon-Shevin (2010) writes:

> The increasing heterogeneity of classrooms—through the movement to fully include students with disabilities and other efforts to desegregate classrooms previously divided by race, gender, or ethnicity—makes the need for classroom communities even more salient. If we are to have classrooms that not only include students who are diverse in many ways, but also make them welcome, appreciated, and valued members of the classroom environment, we will have to set community building as a high priority. (viii)

Although I have used various enjoyable and entertaining ice-breaking activities in the first few weeks of school, asking them to think and talk about themselves has revealed the most to me about my students and enabled me to build a community of learners quickly. The two tools I use, regardless of grade level, are surveys and interviews. These tools enable the entire community of learners to get to know one another, and from this knowledge engagement begins. When we know who we are, who our peers are, who and what our community represents, and we have set the course for a year of student engagement!

Student Surveys

Surveys reveal the most about students when they uncover information about student interest, efficacy, and identity.

Living in today's world, many of us have become skeptical of surveys. Every time we turn around, someone else is asking for our opinion of a product or an experience. Yet for our students, a survey is a novel and exciting tool that will get them thinking and sharing things about themselves.

The key to successful surveys is to make them pointed enough to glean the information we are looking for and short enough to keep students' interest. The best ones focus on the three domains of student engagement: **behavioral, emotional**, and **cognitive**. Ming-Te Wang and Jacquelynne Eccles (2013) state: "In order to promote school engagement, we must first better understand the school factors that influence student engagement." Student surveys should ask questions related to these factors. (Examples are provided in Figures 2.3 and 2.4.)

SAMPLE QUESTIONS FOR A K–2 SURVEY

- What is your favorite thing to do in school?
- What do you like most about school?
- Who is someone you like to work with while playing or learning?
- What do you do when you don't understand something at school?
- Do you like to share ideas with others?
- Do you always follow school rules?

Name _____ Date _____

Use drawing and writing to answer the following questions.

What is your favorite thing to do in school?	
What do you like most about school?	
Who is someone you like to work with while playing or learning?	

Use a 🙂 😐 🙁 *to answer the following questions.*

| Do you like to share ideas with others? | |
| Do you always follow school rules? | |

Figure 2.3 Sample K–2 Student Survey

Name _____	Date _____
Question	**Student Response**
What do you like most about school?	
Whom do you like to work with on school assignments and projects?	
What about learning excites you?	
What strategies do you use that help you with your school work?	
What strategies do you use when learning gets hard?	
Are you able to finish school tasks on time?	
Do you always complete your homework?	
Do you like to participate in class discussions? Why or why not?	

Figure 2.4 Sample 3–8 Student Survey

Peer Interviews

Asking and answering questions is an important skill for all learners to cultivate. One of my favorite setting-the-course activities is having students interview each other: they get to know each other on many different levels and in turn get to know themselves. Answering questions about themselves and their learning helps them build a learning identity.

I begin by demonstrating how an interview is conducted and explaining that the questions can focus on a particular discipline (science, math, literacy) or deal with learning in general. Then I let students have a crack at it. (One year my fourth graders interviewed each other about their reading and writing preferences, struggles, and goals. Questions ranged from what they liked to read and write about to where they liked to read and write to pieces they had written or books they had read to genre preferences to strategies they used as readers and writers. See Figure 2.5a and 2.5b.)

Figure 2.5a Sample Student Interview

When the interviews have been completed, I have students use what they've learned to write a short biographical sketch about their interview partner. This may be accompanied by a photograph or some other visual image that represents the person.

Each of these community-building tools—surveys and interviews—enables the entire community of learners to get to know each other. It is from this knowledge that engagement begins. When we know who we are, who our peers are, who and what our community represents, we are on the right path and have set the course for a year of student engagement!

Millie

Millie likes to read and write. Millie likes fiction better than nonfiction. Sometimes Millie use her imagination but not all the time. Millie likes to write about animals.

Millie likes to read long chapter books and series. Millie sometimes reads classics, but not all the time. Millie likes to read difficult books. Millie doesn't like wars and scary books.

Millie has a journal. Millie likes to write on her bed every night. When she writes in bed she like to write about her day.

Alexi-

Figure 2.5b Sample Student Interview

Setting the Course Checklist

Developing Classroom Routines

☐ Classroom Meetings
  - ☐ Will you begin or end your day with a daily meeting?
  - ☐ What specific components will you incorporate into this daily meeting (e.g., a read-aloud, the daily schedule, class news)?
  - ☐ Will you have a weekly meeting?
  - ☐ What specific components will you incorporate into this weekly meeting (e.g., celebrating accomplishments, addressing issues, sharing reflections)?

☐ Student Talk
  - ☐ What routines or procedures will you use to encourage student talk (e.g., turning and talking, using nonverbal signals, manipulating objects to add a kinesthetic element to contributing to a conversation)?
  - ☐ How will you balance talk between teacher and students and student to student?

☐ Transitions
  - ☐ Will you use transitions to move students from one activity, period, or aspect of learning to another?
  - ☐ What will your transitions include? Movement? Music? Food?

Building Community

☐ Student Surveys
  - ☐ Will you use a survey to ask students about their attitude toward school, their work habits, how they work through difficulty, and how they feel about collaboration?
  - ☐ Will your survey focus on behavioral engagement? Emotional engagement? Cognitive engagement? All three?

☐ Peer Interviews
  - ☐ Will you use interviews to build community, highlight student interests, and enable students to get to know one another?

Chapter *Three*

Ongoing Assessments That Engage Students

Malachi is sitting in the back of the classroom, his head usually down, only sometimes facing the board, never making eye contact with the two teachers in his collaborative classroom. He seldom has his materials in order and completes about half the work his peers do. He will talk to and engage with his teachers one-on-one, but seldom participates in a class discussion (and never without direct prompting). Most of the time he does not participate in collaborative groups, but occasionally he will contribute a personal story somewhat related to a topic or exercise. He has yet to complete homework.

James is sitting in the front of the classroom, compliant, kind, seemingly observant. James comes to school every day, on time. In class, he faces the teacher, appears to be listening, and is never overtly off task. He doesn't contribute to class conversations and has many questions about independent practice. He seldom expresses excitement about or interest in topics or subjects. He completes homework (although his parents say it's a struggle) and constantly expresses his dislike for school. He's always asking why he is learning something or why he needs to complete a task or project.

James and Malachi are disengaged students. There are many variations of Malachi and James in our classrooms, all students at risk. Yes, at risk. Cognitive, behavioral, emotional, and motivational engagement is crucial to understanding and academic achievement, as is the attitude a student has toward learning (Kush and

Watkins 1996). Some disengaged students may appear cooperative and compliant, but their attitude toward learning is negative and their achievement and enjoyment is severely impaired.

Unfortunately, we all know what disengagement looks like.

Riya comes to school each day with a smile. She is an active learner, interacting with her peers and teachers the moment she walks into a classroom. She is a good community member, reaching out to others in need and helping with classroom logistics. She consistently pushes herself. She doesn't always get everything right, but she perseveres and wants to learn. She is also very aware when learning is hard for her, and she has some good strategies for getting past difficulty.

Christopher is a quiet force in the classroom. He is not overt about his feelings about learning, but he is on task, actively paying attention in whole-class and small-group sessions. He is reluctant to share unprompted during whole-class discussions but interacts and voices opinions when asked. He is often a leader in collaborative situations. He knows a lot about specific subjects and learning in general. He is curious about many topics and is good at managing his time and materials. He completes his work on time; when it needs revision or elaboration, he approaches the task seriously and with purpose.

Riya and Christopher are engaged learners. As teachers, we want and need to cultivate a similar engagement in all of our students. In order to do so, Tristan de Frondeville (2009) encourages us to cultivate what he calls our "engagement meter":

> Be acutely aware of when your students are paying strong attention or are deeply engaged in their tasks. Master teachers create an active-learning environment in which students are on task in their thinking and speaking or are collaboratively working close to 100 percent of the time. Such teachers notice and measure not only when students are on task but also the quality of their engagement.

Therefore, we need to determine the level of engagement our students have, as well as their strengths and weaknesses with regard to engagement. I do this with the help of three types of assessments:

1. diagnostic engagement assessments
2. ongoing appraisals: engagement checks
3. milestone assessments.

● DIAGNOSTIC ENGAGEMENT ASSESSMENTS

Engagement is essential to learning and crucial to students' success. Engagement is the key attribute of a successful learner, and its lack is perhaps the most important reason learners struggle. Many factors contribute to disengagement: not understanding the material, not having the skills needed to succeed, and even the perception of failure.

All learners, all human beings, have both the capacity for and experience with engagement. The key is to uncover when and under what conditions a learner is or can be engaged. Adam Reger (2013), commenting on the Wang and Eccles (2013) research, writes:

> [T]he study . . . suggests that student engagement—essential for success in school—is malleable, and can be improved by promoting a positive school environment. The result paves the way for future work to offer teachers diagnostic tools for recognizing disengagement, as well as strategies for creating a school environment more conducive to student engagement.

Engagement is malleable. Teachers can assess and then cultivate engagement.

Therefore, after I've evaluated my getting-to-know-you surveys and interviews, I "diagnose" students' level of engagement and determine their strengths and weaknesses (or what I like to call "next steps") as learners.

Considering strengths is important, and I'll use a personal experience to explain why. A few years ago, I decided I needed a new physical activity in my life, one I would enjoy and that fit my lifestyle. I chose yoga. Although my previous participation in sports had prepared me for the rigor yoga requires and helped me acquire some of the necessary skills, I had never taken a yoga class. At the beginning, I was very aware that I had never done yoga and was frankly a bit out of shape. So the yogi and I explored my strengths and weaknesses. What kind of muscle memory did I have? What parts of my body were strong? Legs? Arms? Core? I have great balance, and that entered the equation. However, I was in my forties, hadn't exercised with any regularity in quite a while, had lost muscle strength, and have a metabolic disorder. It would have been easy to see only my weaknesses; however, to create an exercise plan that would work for me, we needed to see my strengths.

Surveys and interviews explored in Chapter 2 are the first step to assessing and cultivating engagement.

Evaluating learners' level of engagement, their strengths that support engagement, and their weaknesses or areas of disengagement allows us to tap into what is already working. Understanding students' strengths in the context of their motivation to learn, their level of engagement, and their overall attitude toward learning allows us to position them to achieve and improve. All learners need to be positioned for success.

For many years, teachers and schools looked at engagement only in terms of school behavior. "In the past, only behavioral measures of student engagement—such as class attendance, turning in homework on time, and classroom participation—had been evaluated when gauging student engagement" (Reger 2013). A diagnostic tool needs to combine all three elements of engagement—behavioral, cognitive, and emotional—to diagnose the level of engagement, recognize strengths, and illuminate weaknesses. One such tool that will identify student engagement and build our engagement meter is provided in Figure 3.1.

Diagnostic tools should consider the three elements of engagement: behavioral, cognitive, and emotional.

Student _____ **Date** _____

1. Does the learner appear connected and engaged or disconnected and disengaged during learning? On a scale of 1–5 (1 being the lowest and 5 the highest), rate the learner's level of engagement.

    1   2   3   4   5

2. Provide one or two specific examples of engagement and one or two specific examples of disengagement.

    _____

    _____

    _____

3. When do you most see this behavior?

    ☐ Whole-class settings

    ☐ Small-group settings

    ☐ When working independently

4. Is the learner actively involved in learning? Does the learner plan for and initiate learning?

    Yes   No

    Provide examples: _____

    _____

    _____

5. In what is the learner interested? Identify subjects and topics by which the learner is excited.

    _____

    _____

    _____

Figure 3.1 Engagement Diagnostic Assessment

This three-part diagnostic tool provides a quick read on a student. The scale in question 1 measures the learner's engagement level. Successful learners have moderate (3) to high (5) levels of engagement. The follow-up questions ask you to document concrete examples of engagement or disengagement so you can determine which learning settings work best for the learner and use them to cultivate ongoing engagement. The second question investigates cognitive strengths or weaknesses for learning. Reflection, planning, and self-regulation are all key factors of engagement; you need to know whether a learner has those cognitive qualities. The third question is strengths based. Every learner is engaged and excited by something, although she or he may not demonstrate this excitement in class. For example, Malachi loves car racing and professional basketball. He is actually a history buff, and his favorite periods in history are the Civil War era and the Civil Rights movement. He is not always engaged in English or social studies class but will connect in small groups that are investigating or reading about these eras. Only through surveys and a diagnostic tool was this revealed. After you have completed this diagnosis, you can use the chart in Figure 3.2 to consider next moves.

IF . . .	THEN . . .
If the learner scores a 1 or 2 on the engagement scale . . .	Design an engagement plan of action or intervention plan to increase learner engagement. (Specific examples are provided later in this chapter.)
If the learner scores a 3, 4, or 5 on the engagement scale . . .	Use specific examples of engagement and learner interests to create future learning contexts. These contexts should consider and utilize structures, materials, and interests that engage him or her.
If disengagement occurs in whole-class settings . . .	Consider ways to increase engagement in this environment: • Move the learner's seat closer to you and lesson materials. • Introduce nonverbal signals to the learner and incorporate them into the lesson. • Individually acknowledge the learner's participation, completion of assignments, academic success, and so on.
If disengagement occurs in small-group settings . . .	• Use a survey like those discussed in Chapter 2 to determine the best collaborative partners for this learner. • Reconfigure groups to provide peers that are a better match.

(continues)

(*continued*)

If disengagement occurs during independent practice . . .	• Be sure your expectations are clear and the learner has them in writing. • Set short-term goals. Provide the learner with direct and positive feedback for shorter periods of time. • Allow the learner time each day to craft individual "I will" learning statements, thus increasing ownership of daily independent learning.
If the learner is not actively involved in learning . . .	Provide tools to build self-regulation: • weekly activity chart • weekly planner for homework assignments • positive reinforcement charts • goals conference based on the learner's weekly meeting reflection.

Figure 3.2 If–Then Chart

ONGOING APPRAISALS: ENGAGEMENT CHECKS

If student engagement is to continue throughout the year, we need to monitor it frequently. This need not be cumbersome or add to current classroom practices. These appraisals, or what I like to call engagement checks, are simple, informative, and seamlessly and naturally integrated into good instruction. They take the guess-work out of understanding and monitoring engagement and thus build our engagement meter. I use three types: checks for understanding, entrance/exit tickets, and reflections.

Checks for Understanding

A check for understanding is more than a formative assessment: we are evaluating and monitoring cognitive engagement. Douglas Fisher and Nancy Frey (2011) discuss the connection between checking understanding and monitoring student learning:

> What does quality checking for understanding look and sound like? Our analysis of classroom instruction and assessment suggests that teachers can check for understanding in several ways, including the use of oral language, questioning, writing, projects and performances, and tests. When teachers use those procedures, they know which students understand the content and which students need additional instruction.

The best ways to check for understanding and overall continued cognitive engagement are through nonverbal language, oral questioning, and written responses. Written responses are an essential tool for developing and checking understanding, and work particularly well for students who are uncomfortable sharing thoughts orally. Some strategies are suggested next.

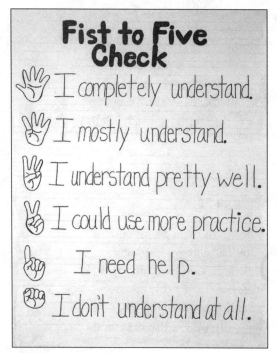

Figure 3.3 Fist to Five Class Chart Example

Fist to Five

This strategy is a way for students to communicate their level of engagement and understanding nonverbally and kinesthetically. A fist, or zero fingers, indicates no understanding. Five fingers indicate total engagement and complete understanding. Four fingers represent a good deal of understanding. Three fingers indicate partial understanding; the student needs to be pulled back into the lesson. One or two fingers means the student needs redirection and help. See Figure 3.3.

Thumbs Up, Thumbs Down, Thumbs to the Side

This is another kinesthetic strategy. Thumbs up is a positive response—you understand, you are still with us, you agree. Thumbs down means the opposite—you do not understand, you are lost or confused, you disagree. Thumbs to the side conveys anything that falls in between. For example, when I asked a group of fifth graders if they were following the historical passage we were close reading, some students used a thumb to the side to indicate they were having trouble understanding. (Thumbs to the side can also indicate you're not sure.) I explain to the students that they are communicating just with me—thumbs in front of them, not high in the air—so everyone can communicate authentically, without embarrassment.

Oral Strategies/Whip-Around

What's most important with oral strategies is ensuring full participation. Having students raise their hand has never worked for me. Only those few highly motivated students raise their hand; the others check out. Whether the strategy is old school (drawing name-labeled popsicle sticks from a can or jar, for example) or uses the latest technology (an interactive whiteboard program like The Hat), students need to be called on randomly, be given time to rehearse, and be allowed time to form a response. I also allow students to pass if they need more time to think or aren't comfortable sharing at that moment.

My favorite oral engagement check is the whip-around—a quick oral response from each student. I vary the order. If they're seated in a circle, I may start at my right or my left. It students are at their seats, I may ask them to respond by row or table or alphabetically. The more creatively you can trigger random responses, the better. Sometimes I gauge the room and start with students who I know will be most comfortable sharing in the particular context.

Jot Something

My favorite written strategy is having students jot something down—in a notebook, on a sticky note, on a whiteboard—related to our lesson or conversation. In particular, primary students in grades pre-K–2 respond well to the use of whiteboards. This tool provides the needed spacing and support for jotting when they are at their seat or on a carpet. This strategy gives me a glimpse into their thinking and understanding, and I can make any necessary adjustments. I read the notes over students' shoulders but often collect them as well, so I can evaluate them more thoughtfully as I plan future lessons.

Students can use digital tools such as a Google Doc or note-taking apps like Google Keep, OneNote, or EverNote.

Circle, Triangle, Square

Using symbols works well with reluctant writers. To use this strategy, students will code directly on their work or refer to something they are working on (a text, a math problem, a scientific experiment, their own writing) and use this three-part symbol strategy to communicate with me. A circle indicates they understand or are interested. A square indicates they are confused, not interested, or don't understand. A triangle indicates they have a question (they often include the question after it).

Checks for understanding can be verbal, nonverbal, or written.

Entrance/Exit Tickets

In a post on the ReadWriteThink website (www.readwritethink.org), Cathy Allen Simon and Patrick Striegel write:

> The Exit Slip strategy is used to help students process new concepts, reflect on information learned, and express their thoughts about new information. This strategy requires students to respond to a prompt

given by the teacher, and is an easy way to incorporate writing into many different content areas. Furthermore, the Exit Slip strategy is an informal assessment that will allow educators to adapt and differentiate their planning and instruction.

It's also a great way to monitor interest and understanding. Simply give students a slip of paper (note card, sticky note, etc.) at the beginning or end of a class or learning period and have them answer or respond to a question or a prompt.

Many teachers regard entrance/exit tickets as a formative assessment and/or a check for understanding. I won't argue with that. However, I've given them a category of their own because they should be used often, not as one option in a list of many. They can be collected, posted in the classroom, or retained digitally on a class wiki or blog.

Entrance tickets are filled out and collected at the beginning of a class or learning period. Sample questions and prompts are included here.

SAMPLE ENTRANCE TICKET PROMPTS
Based on yesterday's learning, what do you want to explore today?
What questions do you have about last night's homework?
What interests you most about [the day's topic or content]?

Whatever the prompt, entrance tickets are quick and efficient ways to check the level of readiness (and potential cognitive engagement) of learners. They also enable you to adjust your teaching to their interests or understanding.

Exit tickets are filled out and collected at the end of a class or learning period. Sample questions and prompts are included here.

SAMPLE EXIT TICKET PROMPTS
What do you think was the most important thing you learned today?
What surprised you?
What do you now know that you didn't know at the beginning of today's learning?

(continues)

(continued)

Draw a handprint. In the fingers list five things you learned today.
Do you agree or disagree with today's learning?
Provide a 3-2-1: three things you learned, two questions you have, one thing you want to know more about.

Students can write or draw their responses. This is an excellent opportunity for them to try *microwriting*—that is, to respond ultraconcisely (for example, respond in twelve words or less, convey your thinking in a short poem, or compose a tweet).

Reflections

Reflection not only cultivates self-regulation and metacognition but is an incredibly useful tool for checking engagement. These reflections can be short or long, written daily, weekly, or by unit. They can be about content, process, or project. They can be a response to a prompt or a free-write.

When I use reflection, I do so to check engagement and create understanding, not just check understanding, and I angle it toward behavior, cognitive perseverance, emotion, or interest. When I had my own classroom, I often used reflection at the end of a learning period, asking students what they thought about the process, product, or topic.

SAMPLE REFLECTION PROMPTS
What is working or not working with your [lab, writing piece, book club]?
What is the best thing you did today as a learner?
What do you now think about [your writing topic, the reading thesis/big idea/theme, your scientific hypothesis]?

These questions are open ended and do not have a "right" or "wrong" answer. Their responses helped me evaluate and maintain their level of engagement. In addition, what these questions do is to create a structure for reflection and talk, both between student and teacher and students with other students, and is the difference between what Kylene Beers (2015) calls, "talk that is to check understanding and talk that is to create understanding."

Making reflections public enables the community to share and learn from their peers' learning and engagement. I do this through a process I call "reading into the circle," or a Quaker share. I ask students to find a short segment of their reflection that resonates for them and that they want to share. We sit in a circle so we can all see one another. Without raising their hand, students randomly share the one or two lines they've chosen. If two students start to speak at the same time, one defers, then speaks next. All students contribute, enabling me to check on what is resonating most with each one. Students benefit from one another's thinking, and I have a quick snapshot of student engagement. I can take notes on any of these reflections, but usually take notes on students I want to monitor.

MILESTONE ASSESSMENTS

Periodic milestone engagement assessments are crucial to our instruction and to the feedback we provide students and caregivers. Mariale Hardiman and Glenn Whitman (2014) write, "Another central value of alternative assessments is that they help students learn essential skills for success in today's world—such as critical thinking, problem solving, communication, collaboration, resiliency, and grit." I use milestone engagement assessments several times during the year in a purposeful, time-bound way—for example, at the end of a marking period (quarter or trimester) or a unit of study or learning module. These assessments help me differentiate the way I monitor my students' engagement. I check the progress of significantly disengaged learners more frequently. More frequent assessment of students who, though not disengaged, display signs of inconsistent engagement also makes sense.

Using a milestone checklist divided into whole-class, small-group, and independent learning contexts (see Figure 3.4) helps me capture the information I'm looking for. Recording the date observed and any pertinent observations and comments lets me see trends and patterns in engagement levels in each context.

Milestone checklists can be used differently for different learners. For example, I may use the Whole-Class Checklist for all students at the end of the trimester, but may use the Small-Group Checklist for particular students on a more frequent basis such as the end of a unit.

Assessment is crucial. It enables us to create a continuous and fluid loop of learning from evaluation to cultivation. Imagining that you will assess engagement ensures that your students will be engaged throughout the year. By using diagnostic tools, daily appraisals, and milestone assessments, you will have a crystal clear picture of your students and their engagement in learning. From this, you can cultivate increased and sustained engagement for all learners!

IN WHOLE-CLASS SITUATIONS

Engagement Behavior	Date Observed	Comments
Tracks speaker		
Listens attentively		
Participates in discussions/responds to questions		
Maintains a learning stance (sitting upright, managing materials)		
Demonstrates affect and emotion appropriate to learning context		

IN SMALL GROUPS

Engagement Behavior	Date Observed	Comments
Tracks speaker		
Listens attentively		
Collaborates with peers		
Sustains work load and expected individual level of participation		

DURING INDEPENDENT WORK

Maintains focus	
Manages time	
Completes work	

Figure 3.4 Learning Engagement Behavior Checklist

ENGAGEMENT ASSESSMENT CHECKLIST

Diagnostic Engagement Assessments

☐ Administer Diagnostic Assessments

    ☐ What diagnostic tools will you use to uncover student engagement level, strengths, and areas of need?

☐ Create a Plan of Action

    ☐ How will you use these tools to create an engagement plan of action for each learner?

Ongoing Appraisals: Engagement Checks

☐ Utilize Checks for Understanding

    ☐ What checks for understanding will you use to determine engagement and understanding?

    ☐ Do they include oral, nonverbal, and written methods of communication?

☐ Implement Entrance/Exit Tickets

    ☐ Does learning begin with an entrance ticket?

    ☐ Are exit tickets used to note learning, capture misunderstandings, and provide information on future learning need?

☐ Cultivate Reflection

    ☐ Is reflection used with enough frequency to maintain levels of interest, engagement, and perseverance?

    ☐ Is reflection a ritual that enhances learning?

Milestone Assessments

☐ Administer Milestone Assessments

    ☐ Are milestone assessments used to continually monitor engagement in a variety of time-bound ways (at the end of a unit or marking period)?

    ☐ Are milestone assessments used in a variety of learning contexts—whole-class, small-group, and independent learning?

Chapter *Four*

Engaging Students Through Meaningful Structures in the Classroom

Engagement is cultivated, not taught, but it is cultivated in teaching and learning contexts. It is essential that we utilize the most salient teaching structures that engage all students. An engaged preschool, elementary, or middle school classroom may at first glance resemble organized chaos. Students are in most corners of the room, materials related to literacy, science, and math within grasp. They are deeply involved in their work, consulting notes from the preceding lesson that are projected on the whiteboard. It takes a while to locate the teacher. She is talking with a group of students about their work. Finishing this conversation, she moves to another group, observes for a moment, and joins in, soon becoming integrally involved in their work and conversation.

Classrooms with highly engaged students utilize two seminal twentieth-century theories: cognitive apprenticeship and the gradual release of responsibility.

The workshop environment of the classroom depicted above is grounded in cognitive apprenticeship: guided learning and doing in a real-world context (Collins et al. 1987). Learning is modeled and directed, social and active. The basic instructional strategies are:

- *modeling*—demonstrating the thinking process
- *coaching*—assisting and supporting student cognitive activities as needed (includes scaffolding)
- *reflecting*—self-analysis and assessment

- *articulating*—verbalizing the results of reflection
- *exploring*—forming and testing one's own hypotheses.

(Dennen and Burner 2008, 427)

The four key components on the part of the apprentices are: "(1) situatedness, (2) legitimate peripheral participation, (3) guided participation, and (4) membership in a community of practice" (427).

The engaged classroom also makes use of the gradual release of responsibility, an instructional model developed by P. David Pearson and Meg Gallagher (1983) that establishes a clear trajectory from teaching to learning and from teacher to student (see Figure 4.1). This I-do-we-do-you-do progression from teacher instruction through student understanding ensures that students are directed by explicit teaching and modeling, are given appropriate time for guided practice and scaffolding, and develop autonomy and master concepts and ideas through independent practice. They are involved throughout the process but are guided to independence through instruction and support.

Parallel Teaching Structures

How do teaching and learning in which the teacher is an expert co-learner and the student is an active, engaged apprentice take place? Teaching opportunities fall into one of three categories: instruction given to the whole class, instruction provided to a small group of students, and instruction delivered to an individual. Each context is essential to classroom practice and needs to be examined individually for its instructional value.

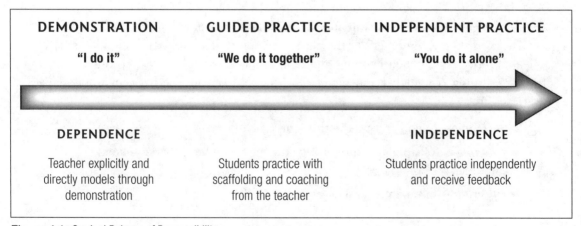

Figure 4.1 Gradual Release of Responsibility

	The Workshop	Whole-Class Instruction	Small-Group Instruction	Individual Instruction	
⇓ COGNITIVE APPRENTICESHIP ⇓	Focused Instruction	Warm up (connect)	Warm up (introduce concept, vocabulary)	Warm up (assess, compliment)	⇓ GRADUAL RELEASE OF RESPONSIBILITY ⇓
		Teach	Teach	Teach	
	Independent Practice and Small-Group Instruction	Try	Try—students try strategy	Try	
	Wrap-up/Share	Clarify	Clarify	Clarify	

Figure 4.2 Parallel Teaching Structures

In addition, all three contexts must also be evaluated collectively to identify parallel components that are most successful in engaging students. (See Figure 4.2.)

Instructional Components

For students to be engaged, instruction must begin with a stage that I refer to as the "warm-up," when students are invited into the learning and the content's relevance is revealed to the learner. Once introduced to the world of teaching by Madeline Hunter (1982) as the "anticipatory set," this is where the objectives of the lesson are connected to the learners in the classroom.

During the warm-up, I always do two things: connect and hook. I want to connect today to yesterday, connect the learner to the content, and gain this learner's immediate interest. In addition, I typically use very similar language at the beginning of each lesson, regardless of the structure, grade level, or content area.

Predictable language and a quest to connect creates initial engagement.

The next part of the instruction—modeling and demonstration—is when I teach. Whatever the grade level or subject area and whether with the entire class, a small group, or an individual learner, I demonstrate a specific strategy, a thinking process, how to use a tool or set of materials, or a method to find information or an answer. The key is teaching by doing, not teaching by talking. I incorporate a personal or student anecdote, model the skill or tool myself, and/or present the work of a student or an adult expert as an example.

Through this active teaching approach, students continue to engage in the lesson.

For example, when teaching middle school students how to compose daily labs for science experiments, I might show them lab notes and reports from scientists at the Lamont Doherty science observatory, highlight key components, and demonstrate how to create these components in their own reports. Or, when teaching students how to demonstrate incorporating transitions in a piece of informational writing, I would articulate aloud my thinking, struggles, and decisions as I inserted transitional words.

During this stage of the lesson, through personal, purposeful, supported, active involvement, students maintain and deepen their engagement.

Trying out the content or skill themselves is the next stage of a lesson and is necessary to maintain student engagement. Essential to learning is the opportunity for students to be actively involved through an opportunity for guided practice, or in other words, the "we do." In a small-group math lesson, I may ask the students to name the steps they will use to solve the next problem. If I am teaching an individual reader to determine the meaning of a word from context and syntax, I have her read the next few sentences and try the strategy out with me. I allow her ample time to grapple with the strategy but assist and join in when necessary.

Through clarification, students are set up to maintain engagement through the remainder of the learning, including the independent practice and ongoing work.

The last part of the lesson is the clarification. Clarifying is key if students are to remain engaged during their independent practice. I have two objectives here: to restate the teaching point and connect to the ongoing work of the learner. In a small-group reading lesson, I would restate what we have just learned—"We can infer the character's motivations through his actions and interactions with others"—and connect it to students' ongoing reading and learning lives—"In your independent reading (or when completing tonight's homework), you will want to read closely the sections describing a character's actions and his interactions with other characters and infer his motivation."

The four components of any lesson, in any discipline, at any grade level, are summarized in Figure 4.3.

One Lesson, Three Structures

All teaching includes the four lesson components. However, a lesson conducted for and with the whole class will have a particular flow, timing, and nuance, as will a lesson with a small group or a conference with an individual. Figure 4.4 outlines the elements of a lesson in each of these structures. The components (warm up, teach, let students try, and clarify), the teaching point, and some of the teaching tools are the same, but there are also differences.

WARM UP

What we do: Connect to previous teaching, connect to the learner, capture students' attention and interest, and activate prior knowledge.

Sample language:

To connect to earlier teaching and to the learner: "Yesterday we investigated our rock specimens and conducted two tests used by geologists, the hardness test and the streak test."

To capture students' attention and activate prior knowledge: "Today, we are going learn another test used by scientists that will enable you to confirm your hypothesis of rock type."

TEACH

What we do: Demonstrate one clear teaching point by sharing a personal or student anecdote, modeling the skill or tool ourselves, and/or using the work of a student or an adult expert as an example.

Sample language:

To signal the teaching point: "Today I am going to teach you how readers/writers. . . ."

To demonstrate the teaching point: "Watch me as I. . . ." "Now look how this reader/writer/scientist. . . ."

LET STUDENTS TRY

What we do: Ask students to envision how their work will go, turn and talk to a partner, or briefly try a strategy together.

Sample language:

"Talk to your partner about how you will. . . ."

"Now, it's your turn to. . . ."

CLARIFY

What we do: Restate the teaching point and connect it to ongoing student work during independent practice.

Sample language:

To restate the teaching point: "Today we learned how to. . . ."

To connect to independent practice: "Today during your independent practice, you will. . . ."

Figure 4.3 Components of a Lesson

WARM UP

What we do: Connect to previous teaching, connect to the learner, capture students' attention and interest, and activate prior knowledge.

Whole Class	Small Group	Individual Conference
"Yesterday we looked at how to include the most pertinent facts in our writing so that the writing is informative to our readers. Today we are going to look at another element in our writing: flow. By looking at flow, we will ensure that we keep our readers interested in our writing and move the writing from idea to idea."	"I've asked for the four of you to meet with me so that we can look at the flow of our writing. Each of you has a strong piece, with a really engaging lead. Your pieces also end nicely, either with an additional anecdote or with a concluding statement that sums up your biggest idea. What we want to ensure is that the material in between flows well."	"Hi, [student name]. I see that you have your first draft down and that your writing incudes many facts and a few definitions that really inform the reader; this is great. What I want us to look at today is how well your writing flows from one idea to the next. Read aloud paragraphs one and two to me and let's notice that."

TEACH

What we do: Demonstrate one clear teaching point by sharing a personal or student anecdote, modeling the skill or tool ourselves, or using the work of a student or an adult expert as an example.

Whole Class	Small Group	Individual Conference
"Today I am going to teach you how to have your writing flow from idea to idea by inserting transitions. A transition is a word that connects one idea to the next and helps the writing flow throughout the piece. Watch as I look at paragraphs two and three and choose a word that will move the writing to the next idea."	"I want us to look at the class writing that we did over the last two days. Watch as I insert a few possible transitions between the second and third paragraph. The third paragraph is really adding on information. Which transitional word would best connect the writing transition here?"	"So we saw how each paragraph, separately, says what you want it to say, but that there doesn't seem to be a strong connection or flow between the two paragraphs. Let me show you how in our anchor text, the writer moves smoothly between paragraph one and two."

LET STUDENTS TRY

What we do: Ask students to envision how their work will go, turn and talk to a partner, or briefly try a strategy together.

Whole Class	Small Group	Individual Conference
"Now that we have examined and discussed my transitions in paragraphs two and three, I want you to begin to imagine the transitional words you will use in your writing. Reread your first and second paragraphs and look at transitional words on our chart. What transitional words might you use?"	"Turn and talk to your partner about which word would work best and sound smoothest. Then use our shared writing to imagine what other transitions are needed between ideas."	"Now I want you to try putting transitions between your first two paragraphs. Let's look at our chart of transitional words. Find a few transitional words that you think will work there and try them out. Let's read that. How does it sound?"

(*continues*)

(continued)

CLARIFY

What we do: Restate the teaching point, and connect it to ongoing student work during independent practice.

Whole Class	Small Group	Individual Conference
"Today we explored how to incorporate transitional words into our writing so that our writing flows from idea to idea. Now, as you work independently, I want you to try out different transitions between ideas. Later, you will share your writing with your writing club to see what transitional words work best."	"Today we worked together to insert transitions into our class writing so that the ideas flowed smoothly. Now I want you to incorporate transitions into your own writing. As you are working, try out your ideas with your partner to get feedback."	"You decided that the word *although* works best as a transition to your second paragraph. Now I want you to look at the rest of the piece to see what other transitional words are needed. I will check back in a little while to see how you're doing."

Figure 4.4 One Lesson, Three Structures

In each structure, the intent of the warm-up is to connect to the content and the learner and to capture the learner's attention. During the whole-class lesson, the connection is made to the class as a community of learners, to the unit of study, and to the content in general as it pertains to their individual writing pieces. The warm-up for the small group is more nuanced, addressing this group of individuals and their particular writing pieces, both strengths and needs. The warm-up for the individual conference is particular to this student and includes a compliment and an assessment of the student's writing.

The intent of the teaching phase is to share and sustain one teaching point through demonstration and modeling. During the whole-class lesson with a large number of students, the teacher demonstrates. During the small-group lesson, there is more opportunity for collaboration; the teaching is more interactive, and the students actively participate. During the conference, the teaching centers on a mentor text. The teacher and student literally hold and notice a text together.

During the give-it-a-try phase in each structure, there is active involvement on the part of the students. As a whole class, the students envision possibilities for their own writing, as the give-it-a-try here needs to accommodate the fact that there are many learners and one teacher. In the small group, where there is greater opportunity for collaboration, student pairs grapple with the class writing. During the conference, the teacher observes, scaffolds, and supports the individual writer, personally and in close proximity.

In the clarification portion of each structure, the teacher reiterates the teaching point. As a whole class, the students then apply the learning independently. In the small group, the students continue to collaborate. During the independent conference, the writer continues to work on her piece of writing.

Whole-class, small-group, and individual teaching contexts are parallel structures that contain four components. Each component works in tandem with the others yet discretely engages students.

● WHOLE-CLASS INSTRUCTION

To ensure engagement during whole-class instruction, we need to consider the length of the lesson and the kinds of materials we use.

Lesson Length and Timing

When I began teaching, lessons were long; students' attention waned, and they had little time for independent practice. Then the minilesson became the big new thing and the focus became: how short could we make it? Five to seven minutes became the standard, regardless of grade level or subject matter. But for optimal teaching and learning, we need to pay attention to the ratio of teacher instruction (I do) and student practice (you do). Brain research reveals that human beings cannot listen attentively for more than twenty minutes at a time. That's a good barometer: because a typical class period, kindergarten through high school, regardless of discipline, is forty-five minutes, this leaves twenty-five minutes for independent practiced and reflection.

If a lesson is *at most* twenty minutes, we need to time the components appropriately. The warm-up and clarification can both be very brief and will benefit from consistent language. During teaching demonstrations, it's easy to tell too many stories or get sidetracked by student questions. Anecdotes and questions are fine, but manage them, and choose one to two to illustrate the point. Managing materials in the lesson also enables time efficiency. If using a text or manipulatives, consider introducing the materials in another structure or time in the day or for older students, have students interact with the materials prior to the lesson for homework or as a do now.

We also need to provide guided practice during the give-it-a-try in a way that doesn't require a lot of time. Having students envision their work allows them to picture themselves using a strategy or method without actually doing so. I often ask students to try a small part of the process with another student. While they are sharing, I listen in. Then, instead of asking for volunteers, I share pertinent examples with the class.

Materials

Without question, materials engage students. The key is to choose the materials wisely. I'll share a cautionary tale related to use of texts. In a fifth-grade classroom I was working in recently, the students were using a story to study elements of narrative; it took place in the seventies with characters and a plot that were no longer relevant, it played with time in a way that was hard to follow, and contained hardly any dialogue. The teacher recognized that the students were bored and apathetic. Therefore, the teacher and I brainstormed a list of more appealing narrative subgenres, as well as the kinds of characters and plot elements and conflicts her students would find interesting. We came up with two texts—*Wonder*, by R. J. Polacio, and the picture book *Dad, Jackie, and Me*, by Myron Uhlberg. Both texts fit the complexity requirements for the unit and exhibited the narrative elements the students needed to examine. What was different was how much these new texts resonated with the students; both texts contained a diversity of characters whose experiences appealed to the students.

Beyond text choice, we also need to consider the visual and tactile appeal of materials. I pull a lot of images from the Internet and project them on an interactive whiteboard. This is especially helpful to second language learners and students with learning differences. When appropriate, I also put actual objects into students' hands: a hard copy of the text, a protractor, a streak plate.

Materials for whole-group instruction should meet the following criteria:

- Do they resonate with students on a personal level?

- Are they culturally relevant, relevant to the topic, or both?

- Do they contribute a visual element to the learning?

- Do they add a tactile element to the lesson? Can students manipulate them?

> *When conducting* whole-class lessons, the key to building and maintaining engagement is to consider lesson timing and materials.

INDEPENDENT PRACTICE

In using the theories of cognitive apprenticeship and gradual release of responsibility, the next component of a workshop or apprenticeship model is independent practice, the component of learning where students move from an instructional context to a place of independence and practice.

During this time, students practice the skills, strategies, habits, and processes that matter most in the discipline: reading, writing, computing, solving, creating, hypothesizing, researching, and, in essence, doing. During independent practice, students work within the confines of both the content of the curriculum and the content of their own learning. This means that classrooms that use this instructional approach provide the space and time for students to practice what was taught in the lesson and work on what they need and want related to their own learning.

To make this manageable, I implement what I call the "practice percentage rule." For me, for 75 percent of the independent practice time students work in ways that further their own learning (reading their own texts, working on self-selected projects, challenging themselves with math algorithms, games, or projects, etc.) and 25 percent of time, they work on practice related to the lesson. The magic is not in the percentage but in the belief that both matter: the content of the lesson and the content of the student.

To enable independent practice, and to sustain independent practice that enables students to grow and develop as learners, teachers then move to a place of continued support, using the structures of small groups and conferring. During this time of instructing students in small groups and individually, teachers are supporting, facilitating, and coaching as necessary.

SMALL-GROUP INSTRUCTION

Small-group instruction is powerful. Kimberly D. Tanner (2013) writes:

> To promote an inclusive community within the classroom, instructors can integrate opportunities for students to work in small groups during time spent within the larger class. For some students, participation in a whole-group conversation may be a persistently daunting experience. However, instructors can structure opportunities for such students to practice thinking and talking by regularly engaging students in tasks that require students to work together in small groups.

During small-group instruction, students are engaged through teacher coaching, use of collaboration, and differentiating needs.

Through small-group instruction, we are able to adapt two things: our instructional moves and our objectives to specific learners with common learning needs. This enables us to acknowledge and address the differences each student brings to the table. Carol Ann Tomlinson (2014) writes:

> Teachers in differentiated classrooms begin with a clear and solid sense of what constitutes powerful curriculum and engaging instruction. Then they ask what it will take to modify that instruction so that each learner comes away with understandings and skills that offer guidance to the next phase of learning. Essentially, teachers in differentiated classrooms accept, embrace, and plan for the fact that learners bring many commonalities to school, but that learners also bring the essential differences that make them individuals. Teachers can allow for this reality in many ways to make classrooms a good fit for each individual. (4)

Figure 4.5 Differentiating Through Small-Group Instruction

When planning our small-group instruction, we want to maximize opportunities for student collaboration and differentiation (Figure 4.5).

Collaboration

Classrooms are social places. In any social context, there is the ability for students to collaborate—on ideas, assignments, and on projects. Not only is collaboration naturally and readily available to a small group of learners, but collaborations skills are essential to develop.

In a recent survey (Palmisano 2010), fifteen hundred of the world's CEOs, when asked what they look for in future leaders, said it is the ability to be collaborative—to work alongside others, melding ideas, and creating new thinking in a shared way. Collaboration is not only necessary for future success in school and the workplace but also a highly effective way for students to learn and deepen their understanding. When students collaborate, they are most engaged.

Collaboration is also endorsed by the Common Core State Standards. The speaking and listening standards in all grades seek to develop communication and collaboration skills. Anchor standard 1, in the communication and collaboration portion of the listening standard, reads, "Prepare for and participate effectively in a range of conversations and collaborations with diverse partners, building on others' ideas and expressing their own clearly and persuasively." From kindergarten through high school, our students are expected to share ideas, pose questions, and accept and acknowledge the ideas of others. Small-group instruction is our opportunity to have them do just that.

To foster collaboration in small-group instruction, we need to answer these questions:

- What opportunities for collaboration exist in this small group?
- How will we use collaboration in the demonstration part of the group lesson?
- Can students try the strategy collaboratively? Independently first, then collaboratively?
- What element of collaboration will carry over into independent practice?

In the example in Figure 4.4, the teacher has the students help her decide what transition words to use in her demonstration; the students turn and talk while they are trying out transitional words; and they work with a partner during independent practice. This high level of collaboration is extremely engaging: it is hard to disconnect when you are working actively.

Differentiation

The teaching point for a whole-class lesson is chosen based on standards related to a specific curriculum. But students also need additional and alternative teaching points connected to them as learners. This element of differentiation is built specifically and purposefully into a small-group lesson. Each student in need of a particular teaching point is gathered in a small group, and the lesson is delivered collaboratively. The key to grouping students effectively is identifying common needs. Who needs work with transitional words? Who has an engaging lead but a blasé ending? Who understands mode but not median? Who is having difficulty summarizing findings from the lab?

A chart like the one in Figure 4.6 helps us track our students' discrete skills and easily see who needs help with what.

INDIVIDUAL INSTRUCTION

One-to-one conferences with students are most commonly thought to take place during literacy instruction, but they are a valuable form of instruction in any discipline. I've had conferences with students in math, science, and history. A conference is the ultimate form of differentiation. The teaching point is related to the

Student Name	Skill or Strategy									

Figure 4.6 Class Skills/Strategy Grid

curriculum's goals and objectives but is pertinent to something with which a specific learner is struggling or excelling. We come to a conference knowing what we might teach the learner (a chart like the one in Figure 4.6 enables us to do that), but also with the understanding that we will choose the specific teaching point as we are meeting with the learner. The lesson format has some minor variations from whole-class and small-group instruction as students benefit from specific feedback to the learner during the assess and compliment stage, proximity to the teacher and materials, and the strategy of the teacher being a perfect partner.

Assess and Compliment

The intent of the warm-up—to connect to the learner, connect to the lesson, and capture the learner's attention—is the same, but I do so by complimenting the learner and conducting some research. Let's say I'm having a reading conference with Evan, a fifth grader who is having difficulty summarizing a text.

I begin with a compliment that is authentic and related to the teaching I intend to do. "Hi, Evan, how is your reading going today?" Evan, with a shy smile and a shrug, says, "Great." I barrel on, not letting myself be thrown by not really getting an answer. "I'm going to talk to you today about something we all need to do as good readers, but I want to begin by saying how impressed I've been with your book choices lately. Picking books that are important and connected to us means the work we have to do as readers will come naturally. We have to feel connected to what we are reading to understand either a section or the entire book well enough to summarize it. I want us to talk about what's involved in summarizing and see whether I can help you create summaries at the end of a few chapters."

I also want to conduct some research about what exactly is getting in Evan's way. I begin with the obvious, asking how it is going and what feels good and what feels challenging. "Your teacher and I have noticed that summarizing seems hard for you, especially when you are asked to do it in writing. It feels different from the conversations you have with your reading partner and your contributions to class discussions. Any idea what's going on?"

"Well, I feel like I can talk about a chapter or part right after I read it, and that is when I am talking to my partner or when we are talking as a class. But when I am asked to write a summary, I forget exactly what happened. Also, I am not sure what to put in and what to leave out."

In this is the warm-up, I have:

- connected Evan to the content
- connected him to the teaching point

- complimented him
- found out the specific difficulty he has with summarizing.

Evan is ready to benefit from my one-to-one teaching.

Proximity

As I mentioned in Chapter 1, our position in relation to our learners—where we stand, where they sit—makes a significant difference in how carefully and closely they attend to our instruction. In a conference, we have direct proximity with the students, sitting either across or beside them (see Figures 4.7 and 4.8). There is no right or wrong choice, but it should be a thoughtful decision. The benefit of sitting across is that you can look directly at the learner. This really engages some students. You model making eye contact and can interpret and demonstrate nonverbal communication. It may also enable you to have materials between you that will engage the learner.

In my conference with Evan, I sat beside him because I wanted to be able to place text where both of us could read and handle it at the same time. "So, Evan, those are some smart things you understand about yourself and summarizing. Let's

Figure 4.7 Sitting Beside a Student in a Conference

Figure 4.8 Sitting Across from a Student in a Conference

explore that further by looking at a recent summary you wrote." I placed it in front of us. "Let's look at this together and notice what you did. What do you notice?"

"Well, I have the beginning of the book here."

"Can you point to it?" He did, saying that he had included three details in the first paragraph and two in the second paragraph but didn't know whether he should have included any of them. Being able to point to and examine the parts he was referring to was very powerful.

I take full advantage of this component in individual conferences. We point to, highlight, and even cut up text. We handle math manipulatives, and I frequently adjust how a student holds the ruler or uses the protractor. I have students show me how they conducted part of an experiment or point to the evidence in a lab report. Proximity matters and engages!

Being the Perfect Partner

Early in my teaching career, I was fortunate to work with an amazing mentor, Shirley MacPhillips, who gave me some great advice that impacted my teaching profoundly. One day she was in my classroom watching me teach. After observing my lesson and a few conferences, she pulled me aside. "Patty, we know you are the teacher. You stand in front of the room and your name is on the door. But when you are conferring with students, I want you to speak to them learner to learner, reader to reader, scientist to scientist. You will be able to help them and teach them in a way that will resonate with them much more strongly than if you speak to them teacher to student." At the time I wasn't quite sure what she meant, but I took her advice and have been passing it along ever since.

In your conferences, be the perfect partner to your students. Talk to them as a co-learner who has the same struggles. Show them what you would do as a scientist or how to approach something as a mathematician. This not only teaches them, it engages them—they can see themselves doing what you are doing and are ready and willing to stay with you during the conference and go back to their work when you leave.

My conference with Evan continued. "Evan, I struggle with this myself. We always joke that I have a lot to say and I have to make sure my lessons and my writing do not go on too long. The same is true of my summaries. Here is what I do." I showed him the summary I had written for the class as a model the day before. "You see here how I start with a big idea statement and then move on to a few examples in each paragraph? Well, the way I keep myself in check is by writing in the margins as I read a text. I jot a list in the margins of all the parts that could be included in the summary. Here is my list for this summary. See how there are many more things I could have included?" I take the list and hold it next to the big idea statement. "If it fits and goes with it, I put it in the summary. If it doesn't, I don't. Let's try that with your summary. Share your thinking out loud, and I'll jot down a few things that can be included in your summary after your big idea statement." Evan mentioned several plot elements and, like a great partner, I jotted them down. "Now, let's try to imagine which ones belong."

A perfect partner. Perfect in that I was just like him, perfect in that I modeled for him and then supported him as he tried out the strategy, and perfect in that I got out of the way so he could continue his work independently!

Classroom Structures Checklist

Parallel Teaching Structures

☐ Do your whole-class lessons, small-group lessons, and one-to-one conferences follow the same format?

    ☐ Warm up.

    ☐ Teach.

    ☐ Let students try.

    ☐ Clarify.

Whole-Class Instruction

☐ Do you use whole-class teaching when it is most appropriate?

☐ Are your lessons no less than five minutes and no more than twenty minutes?

☐ Do you deliver each part of the lesson in the most efficient and timely manner?

☐ Are lesson materials engaging and used efficiently?

☐ Do your lessons include visual aids?

☐ Are there opportunities in the lesson for students to handle materials?

Independent Practice

☐ Is there time for independent practice each day?

☐ Are students involved in independent practice for at least 60 percent of the learning time? For example, for 25 minutes in a 45 minute period.

☐ Is the independent practice related to both the lesson and related to the learner (the content of the lesson and the content of the learner)?

Small-Group Instruction

☐ Do you use small-group instruction to meet the needs of various learner cohorts?

☐ Does your small-group instruction include collaboration between you and your students?

☐ Does your small-group instruction include collaboration between students?

☐ Do you use small-group instruction to differentiate learners' needs?

☐ Do you use charts and grids to track and identify students' needs?

Individual Instruction

☐ Do you use individual learning conferences to teach and engage learners?

☐ Do you assess and compliment the learner during the warm-up?

☐ Do you optimize proximity to the student and to materials during the conference?

☐ Do you speak to students as a perfect learning partner, learner to learner?

Chapter

Five

Choice as a Principle of Engagement

It's February and the book clubs in Brigid McKenna and Steven Tesher's eighth-grade English classes are reading and discussing books that are part of a trimester module titled "The Self as a Member of a Community in Crisis." The texts and the unit are generating a lot of interest and involvement. Grace is reading *The Book Thief* and thinking about her upcoming project, a music video illuminating the themes of the story and the journey of the characters. She had two other options, a movie trailer or a photo essay. She was intrigued by all of them but chose the music video as the best medium for presenting the themes and images that resonated with her. Having the choice made a big difference in the work she did and with the connection she felt with the project.

In a recent podcast on BAM! Radio, Daniel Pink (July 8, 2013), an expert in motivation and what motivates and engages learners, talked about three conditions for motivation and engagement: purpose, autonomy, and mastery. To cultivate learning we need to:

- create learning situations and tasks that have an authentic purpose relevant to students and the world
- develop autonomy through tasks and learning that encourage independence and self-reliance
- create learning situations that build mastery and develop content and discipline knowledge, expertise, and proficiency.

These conditions are most successful when they stand on the shoulders of a principle that creates the most engagement in learning—choice. Choice motivates us in ways other conditions do not. When we are given the ability to choose—to make decisions, have options, or just be flexible—we are more likely to be engaged and successful.

Edward Deci and Richard Flaste, in *Why We Do What We Do: Understanding Self-Motivation* (1996), explore the concept of choice and its effects on humans. In one experiment, one group of subjects was allowed to choose a puzzle and how long to spend on it. The other group was assigned a puzzle and given a time limit. The authors write:

> As expected, given that a comprehensive picture was beginning to emerge from all these experiments, the subjects who had been offered the simple choices spent more time playing with the puzzles and reported liking them more than the subjects not offered choice. The opportunity to make even these small choices had made a difference in their experience and had strengthened their intrinsic motivation. (33)

Choice matters. Elliot Washor and Charles Mojkowski (2014) describe ten expectations students have to remain engaged and graduate high school, one of which is choice: "Do I have real choices about what, when, and how I will learn and demonstrate my competence? Do my teachers help me make good choices about my learning and work?" I think about both of these questions often. When I was an early childhood teacher, the number one skill I began to develop in my students was the ability to make choices. For students that age, this choice can be simple. Do I want the green paper or the blue? Do I want to go to the block center or the book nook?

Choice continues to be important in elementary, middle, and high school; in fact, choice has a dramatic effect not only on students of all ages but on all kinds of learners, especially learners who struggle. Based on the research of Powell and Nelson (1997), the clearinghouse website Intervention Central suggests the following:

> Allowing students to exercise some degree of choice in their instructional activities can boost attention span and increase academic engagement. Make a list of "choice" options that you are comfortable offering students during typical learning activities. During independent seatwork, for example, you might routinely let students choose where they sit, allow them to work alone or in small groups, or give them two or three different choices of assignment selected to be roughly equivalent in difficulty and learning objectives.

Choice has its roots in the work of Richard M. Ryan and Edward L. Deci (2000), in which they explored the impact of intrinsic and extrinsic motivators and the differences between them. The authors state:

> In self-definition theory we distinguish between different types of motivation based on the different reasons or goals that give rise to an action. The most basic distinction is between *intrinsic motivation*, which refers to doing something because it is inherently interesting or enjoyable, and *extrinsic motivation*, which refers to doing something because it leads to a separable outcome. Over three decades of research has shown that the quality of experience and performance can be very different when one is behaving for intrinsic versus extrinsic reasons. (55)

The connection here is that choice builds intrinsic motivation and in turn leads to greater levels of student engagement. Choice as a basic classroom principle motivates students and builds a greater desire to learn—to persevere, to develop projects and assignments that are complex and thorough, to think critically about ideas.

Tony Wagner, educator, Harvard fellow, and author of *The Global Achievement Gap* among many other works, talks about this connection as well. In a speech he gave at Google headquarters in March 2012, he talks about the three P's that build intrinsic motivation—play, passion, and purpose:

> I discovered that every single one of these young innovators whom I profiled from both advantaged and disadvantaged backgrounds was intrinsically motivated. And then when I looked at what their parents and their teachers had done, they too were very focused on intrinsic motivation. Radically at odds with the culture of schooling, which is all about carrots and sticks. A's and F's and pizza on Fridays if you get good test scores. So what do these parents do? What do these teachers do? There was a pattern of [from] play, to passion, to purpose; parents encouraging much more exploratory, discovery-based play; simple toys—sand, blocks, clay, water, paint, Lego toys as they got older; toys without batteries. They limited screen time. They actively encouraged their kids to find and pursue a passion. They gave them a rich buffet of things to try out—making sure though, that they didn't overschedule their kid's times. So the kids still had time for more discovery-based play. But they encouraged them to try instruments or Scouts or sports or whatever. Not insisting that they put in 10,000 hours to become absolutely excellent at it,

but that they really give it a try and see if it's something they're interested in. These parents as well as the teachers believed it was more important that these kids find and pursue a passion than that they simply achieve academically for its own sake. Teachers building time into every single unit of study where students could investigate, explore, create, invent, ask a question. And you know, the 20 percent time here at Google comes immediately to mind, 'cause I think the best teachers build 20 percent time into each one of their classes. To ensure that students have that time to explore, invent, and create. I wonder, what would happen if we said, "Why shouldn't every teacher have 20 percent time to pursue his or her passions in the context of teaching and learning?"

At his high school, Tony instituted "Google Fridays" when students are given time to play with a purpose, time to choose learning activities and topics that they most want to explore, just like Google employees, who spend 20 percent of their time on topics and projects of their choice. Time to play with purpose and passion leads to deep learning and engagement in the classroom and to innovation and advancement in life.

Teacher Deidra Gammill (2014) introduces a similar structure to her high school students, giving them time each Thursday to research and learn about a topic of their choice. She sets parameters and expectations and shares some of her concerns:

I'll admit—letting go and relinquishing control was scary. Giving students freedom is risky. What if they waste time? What if they don't use the resources responsibly? What if they are really watching YouTube videos and pretending to learn? These are very real concerns, because some kids will do exactly that. But most of them won't. And, frankly, I was tired of limiting the majority in an attempt to control a few. Sharing control of the learning process with my students showed them that I trusted them and respected them as fellow learners. I found that my students responded to that trust and respect by doing what I expected of them, and my classroom became more student-centered and less teacher-centered.

Choice makes a difference. It builds intrinsic motivation in students, has a profound impact both in school and in life, and leads to much higher levels of student engagement. So what's holding us back? We need to imagine choice inside our classrooms in ways that will have the desired impact and be something we can manage. The key is to consider places and spaces where choice can exist simply and powerfully.

In *The Differentiated Classroom* (2014), Carol Tomlinson creates a matrix for differentiation and names three areas in which teachers can differentiate—content, process, and product (15). She defines these ways in which to differentiate in a blog interview with Larry Ferlazzo (2014):

> Teachers can differentiate content (what students learn or how they get access to information), process (how students make sense of and come to understand content), product (how students show what they've learned), and affect and learning environment (classroom arrangement and climate). Each of these elements can be differentiated in response to student readiness, interest, and/or approach to learning.

The same three lenses can be used to outline places and spaces for choice in school: choice of content (curriculum and materials), choice in process (exercises and tools for learning), and choice of products (projects for both school and home learning and assignments).

CHOICE APPLIED TO CONTENT

We need to think first and foremost about choice in the content our students learn. There are some things about curriculum that are mandated or predetermined: the standards that drive us and our teaching have little to do with choice. They are adopted by states, schools, or learning communities at large and do not leave much room for us to decide expectations for our students. That said, I believe that we teach students, not just lessons, and therefore must consider the many ways that choice can be built into content. One way to offer our students choice is through personalized learning. Not to be confused with differentiated instruction (meeting different learning needs with different cohorts or groups of students) or individualized instruction (customizing learning based on student differences and needs), in personalized learning the learner is allowed to make decisions and has choices in his or her instruction. Barbara Bray defines and explores personalized learning in a 2012 blog post:

> To transform a classroom to a personalized learning environment is challenging. First, you need to know what personalized learning means. . . . Personalized learning is all about the learner, starts with the learner, and means the student drives [her or his] learning. . . . Student voice is difficult to hear in a traditional classroom where the teacher provides direct instruction and curriculum that is either provided for the teacher, adapted by the teacher, or designed by

the teacher. Student choice means students choose how they learn something and, possibly, what they learn.

Personalizing learning makes the mandates we need to follow less cumbersome and dogmatic: there are many places to envision personalizing learning for students by considering choice in relation to specific materials and curriculum as a whole.

Choosing Materials

Take the module "The Self as a Member of a Community in Crisis," which I mentioned in the opening paragraph of this chapter. Steve Tesher and Brigid McKenna made many choices themselves when considering how to integrate the standards they would meet in this module. The first was to divide the module into three smaller units of study. Next, they decided the scope of each unit, from the standards addressed to the specific content connection—World War II—to the lessons, including their pacing and sequence.

> *Choice begins* with the teacher. As teachers we can make decisions on content, pacing, and sequence.

They also built in choice and voice for their students. First were the texts students read (see Figure 5.1). These choices build students' autonomy

Core Text 1 (students self-select from this list)	*The Diary of a Young Girl*, by Anne Frank *Stones in Water*, by Donna Jo Nappoli *Maus I & II*, by Arte Spiegelman *The Book Thief*, by Markus Zusak
Core Text 2	Their choice, from an approved list of books focusing on World War II and the Holocaust
Poetry (selected from this list based on teacher discretion and student interest, read in benchmark whole-class lessons)	"The War Works Hard," by Dunya Mikhail "A Song on the End of the World," by Czeslaw Milosz "Deportation," by Inge Auerbacher "November 9, 1938," by Inge Auerbacher "Something to Remember Me By," by Inge Auerbacher "September, 1939," by W. H. Auden
Nonfiction (selected portions from these books and websites)	*I Am a Star*, by Inge Auerbacher *Hitler Youth*, by Susan Campbell Bartolleti www.USHMM.org www.Remember.org

Figure 5.1 Resources for "The Self as a Member of a Community in Crisis"

as readers but also their autonomy in navigating their learning. All students thrive when given the option to choose reading materials that resonate. When making decisions about the materials students can choose, we need to consider student readiness, student needs, our own discretion and content expertise, and, most importantly, student interest.

> *Allowing students* a choice of reading materials is manageable for teachers and engaging for students.

Mapping Curriculum

The K–12 curriculum in Steve and Brigid's district is built around choice. One suggestion I make to all the schools I work with is to stand on the shoulders of their standards and expectations, envision what they want the shared and guaranteed student experience to be, and then planfully and purposefully integrate choice—for both teachers and students—into the curriculum. Choice is a major tenant that drives the instructional practices of teachers, as well as the curriculum documents. The teachers first created a belief statement characterizing the principles that would guide their instruction, including a balanced literacy approach and cultural relevance. Guiding principles ensure purpose in student learning.

Another suggestion I make to all the schools I work with is that when they create curriculum documents, they illuminate big ideas of teaching that are simple and easy to follow. One way to do this is to create an overview for each unit and/or module—a synopsis of what the teaching will entail that will enable teachers to see at a glance both the instructional goals and materials and, more importantly, the instructional components. This is the overview from a fifth-grade three-month, three-unit module titled "Becoming Literary Readers and Writers":

> Through close reading of various types of literary texts that focus on the theme of "who I am," students will learn the structure and elements of a narrative and be able to use what they've learned to create their own narrative based on a topic of their choice. Students will analyze memoir, drama, fiction, and poetry to determine literary elements and techniques authors use, which include theme, characterization, setting, plot, details, dialogue, imagery, transitional words, pacing, and figurative language. While engaging with these texts, students will quote accurately when explaining what the text says explicitly and when drawing inferences. Through modeling, guided practice, and independent practice, students will identify significant information and write summaries of various narratives for the purpose of comparing and

contrasting literary elements and aspects of style. Students will apply these understandings in their own writing while creating a narrative piece in a format of their choice.

Choice is heavily embedded in these units. Students can choose independent reading texts, writing topics, and narrative formats.

Here's another example, from a tenth-grade module on exposition and narration:

> The module addresses the skills of exposition and narration through readings and writing assignments on the themes of friendship, betrayal, vengeance, and the individual voice. The units will help students understand that human behavior cannot be taken at face value. They will also learn that some people take advantage of others' weaknesses and wreak vengeance for perceived injuries. We will examine the ways in which outside factors shape the individual identity, as well as the ways in which identity is fluid. Assessment choices include performing a tragic scene and writing literary essays and memoirs. Students will also write an expository essay on a topic of their choice.

Choice is embedded in the various assessments and in the topic of the expository essay. In addition, we see the purpose of both the teaching and the learning. Teacher decisions are purposeful and direct, and student learning will have purpose as well.

CHOICE APPLIED TO PROCESS

Student voice and choice can also be embedded in the process of learning. Eric Toshalis and Michael J. Nakkula (2012) point out the impact on engagement:

> One of the most powerful tools available to influence academic achievement is helping students feel they have a stake in their learning. To feel motivated to do something and become engaged in its activity, youth (like adults) generally need to feel they have a voice in how it is conducted and an impact on how it concludes. Time and again, research has shown that the more educators give their students choice, control, challenge, and opportunities for collaboration, the more their motivation and engagement are likely to rise.

In the research quoted above, Toshalis and Nakkula discuss the concept of students as stakeholders and explore the idea of students as partners, leaders, and activists who make decisions in their learning. Students become successful stakeholders and decision makers by choosing learning strategies, specific learning tools, and deadlines for work and assignments.

Choosing Learning Strategies

Learning in all disciplines can be developed through exercises in which students are taught specific strategies. For example, as an upper elementary teacher, I taught my students various writing strategies. They needed to try the strategy on the day I taught it (a "must do") and incorporate it in their writing throughout the week so they would grapple with it and become adept at using it. By the middle of the school year, they had a bank of learning strategies at their fingertips. They then became stakeholders. When composing pieces, I wanted them to have choices and make decisions. For example, they had options for how they would begin: conducting an oral rehearsal in which they talked through, with a partner or to themselves, what they would write; brainstorming a list of ideas in writing, leaving space to develop them; drawing a box at the top of the page and writing down the topic and a big idea statement about it. They made the decision and learned to make it thoughtfully, appropriate to the context.

Or take math. To be proficient in solving math problems, one needs to know what strategy to use when. Students are taught a strategy in a daily lesson, use the strategy that day, and practice it throughout the week, at home and at school. As the year progresses, they acquire a bank of strategies they can choose from. Should I guess and check? Draw a picture? Use an algorithm? Make a table or chart? A combination of any of the above? As with writing, there are multiple strategies that they can use to solve the problem. There isn't necessarily a "right" strategy. They choose the strategy that will work for them—the one that will not only get them the answer but also make them stakeholders in their learning who care deeply about the outcome.

Scheduling Learning Tasks at School and at Home

Student must also be allowed to decide when they will complete a learning task or a homework assignment. This may seem counterintuitive, but students can do this successfully in preschool or grad school.

When I was an early childhood teacher, I let students decide what center they would work in and for how long. They weren't able to tell time but were intuitively able to mark its passage by the structure or quantity of their learning. They would say things like, "I will spend time in the art center, then go to the book nook." "I will make two projects in the art center, then go read three books in the book nook." "I will read with Alyssa in the book nook, then work in the art center until I hear the clean-up song." "I choose the block center and will spend all my time there." This led to a much greater degree of student engagement. Students were thoughtfully planful and made better choices than I might have made for them. They were proud of their choices and felt accountable. They began their learning engaged and sustained it.

With upper elementary and secondary students, I embed choice into my weekly classwork and homework assignments. During the Monday morning meeting, I distribute a list of what needs to be completed by the end of the week. Students then determine how long each assignment will take them and decide on which night they will do which assignment. Sometimes, of course, they need to work within parameters—doing math homework after the related lesson or reading a social studies or science chapter before a class discussion or lab session dealing with that material.

Most students need to learn to calibrate themselves. At first eager beavers will do all their homework on Monday night and procrastinators will put it off until Thursday. But they adjust, learning to make wise decisions that consider the circumstances. They do more work on evenings when they have fewer after-school commitments. They schedule around an after-school job or after-school activities. These are factors we cannot know, control, or manage, but our students can and do. Being able to choose empowers them and makes them much more engaged in their learning. They see the purpose and relevance of classwork and homework. The weekly assignments in Figure 5.2 show the must dos and the options for writing.

Allowing students choice in how they learn something, and when and how they practice, builds both autonomy and mastery.

Using a variation of the weekly checklist for independent learning introduced in Chapter 1, I provide specific options for how to use their time. As noted, knowing the work for the week helps students to manage assignments. More importantly, the choice element enables them to engage in a subject or project in powerful ways. To manage this well, I create very similar choice options in each discipline so that students know what to expect and I do not have to create so many activities. For example, the writing options are standard—I always have an option for additional conferences, an option to study craft, and an option to be playful with writing.

WEEKLY OPTIONS FOR WRITING

Must Do	Choice
Planning: Complete opinion essay planner.	Planning: Confer with your writing partner, or sign up for a conference with me to check in on your essay planner. Writers who want more rehearsal or want to receive feedback during this stage may want to choose this activity.
Drafting: Create a draft of opinion essay. Draft is due by Friday.	Drafting: We have explored many ways to start an opinion essay. In your draft, create two or three possible leads and then choose the one that you feel will work best to start your draft.
Conference: Meet with writing partner. Using our rubric, provide your partner with two compliments and two suggestions for making the draft stronger.	Studying craft: For writers who need further inspiration to begin drafting, or who are stuck somewhere in the draft, you may want to continue our close reading of mentor texts. Browse the unit anchor text basket, choose a text that speaks to you, review our close reading Post-its, and "borrow" some strategies from our fellow writers!

My Writing Schedule for the Week of _____

Day	School	Home
Monday		
Tuesday		
Wednesday		
Thursday		
Friday		

Figure 5.2 Weekly Options for Writing

CHOICE APPLIED TO PRODUCT

Whatever the discipline, students can create many types of products as tangible demonstrations of their learning. The important element is not the product, but its authenticity and the choices embedded in its creation. Stephanie Harvey and Harvey Daniels (2009) see projects as a way to engage students in deep authentic learning:

> It's about combining what we know about the research process, about thinking, and about people working together, to create a structure that consistently supports kids to build knowledge that matters in their lives. It's about reversing the disadvantages of conventional projects and making them into true inquiries where kids work deeply, powerfully and joyfully. (74)

Stevi Quate and John McDermott (2009) lay out a framework they call the "six C's" for instruction. The third *C* is *choice*. They assert that providing students the opportunity to choose will increase engagement but will also require planning and scaffolding: "One of the ways to put students in control of their learning—to build their sense of autonomy—is to ensure that they have voice in their learning. However, choice must be scaffolded and intentional" (8).

It is important to note that choice should be limited and released to students gradually. John Guthrie and his colleagues (2004) see limiting choice as a factor in how successful it is in a learning context. Erika Patall, Harris Cooper, and Jorgianne Robinson (2008) believe that the number of choices and options matter and that more are not better:

> Although motivation theory, as well as American society, has generally assumed that more choice is better, some research has suggested the effect of choice may not be so linear. . . . Conversely, in line with self-determination theory, all else being equal in terms of the nature of the choices provided, if an individual is presented with few options or choices, his or her perception of having experienced choice may not be as pronounced compared to when more options or choices are given. Given both theoretical perspectives, we might expect to find an optimum number of options and choices, in that too many choices may lead an individual to feel overwhelmed, and too few choices may not allow the perception of choice to be realized.

We as teachers are the intuitive decision makers who decide how many choices to offer our students. The key is to find a happy medium, which for me is a range between three and six.

Choosing Project Topics

We all like to choose topics—the topic of conversation, the topic we read about, and so forth. Topic choice is an important project consideration, a pathway to engagement. In an Edutopia blog post Nick Provenzano (2014) writes:

> I've been a big fan of project-based learning for many years now, and I've seen the amazing things that can happen when students are given a chance to show a class what they are capable of doing. At the end of the school year, students are often overloaded with all of the things they've been told they *need* to know. How about if you throw them a curveball and ask them what they *want* to learn?

Name _____		Date _____
Today we will begin planning our end-of-year projects. Begin by creating a list of topics that intrigue you, and then move down the page to eliminate choices that won't work. By the end, you will have the perfect project topic!		
Topics related to my life: hobbies, likes, interests I pursue	Topics related to the world: current events, national incidents, global concerns	Topics related to what we have been studying using books and other material I've read
Look at the lists created above. Which category interests you least or do you know the least about or will be hardest to research and learn about? Put an X through that column.		
Consider the remaining two categories. Choose a topic from *each* category and do a five-minute quick-write about it. Put a star next to the category/topic that feels comfortable for you. Be prepared to share why this category/topic works for you.		
Talk about your five-minute quick-writes with your learning partner. At the end of the conversation, choose the category and topic that works for you.		
Category/Topic Choice:		
Why I Choose This:		

Figure 5.3 Topic Choice Planner for Grades 3–8

The key is to provide direction and context and offer a limited choice, not one so open-ended that it overwhelms. Here is a five-step protocol:

1. Identify the standards that will be covered and the project's objectives. What are your goals?

2. Identify any parameters. Do students need to create something written? Is there a presentation component?

3. Present the project, including the parameters, to students in writing.

4. Teach strategies for choosing a topic, give students time to brainstorm topics they're interested in, and support them as they narrow their choices (a tool for doing this is provided in Figure 5.3 and Figure 5.4).

5. Have students eliminate choices with a peer, choose a topic, and provide the topic to you in writing (through dictating and drawing in an early childhood classroom), along with the rationale and a plan of execution.

| Name _____ | Date _____ |

POSSIBLE TOPICS		
Family	**Hobbies: Things I LIKE to Do**	**School Topics**

Talk about your choices with your learning partner.
Put a * next to the choices you like.
Choose the topic that works for you.

Topic Choice:

Figure 5.4 Topic Choice Planner for Grades K–2

Choosing Project Form

Allowing students to choose the form of the project also contributes to high levels of engagement and successful completion. In their "The Self as a Member of a Community in Crisis" module discussed earlier, Brigid McKenna and Steve Tesher offered students choices in the form their final project could take:

> Our next task is to share our understanding and learning with others through images beyond the printed page. You may choose one of three ways to convey the story you saw in your mind and share your ideas about the conflicts of the time period:
>
> - a photo essay
> - a book trailer
> - a thematically connected music video.

Students are able to find a form that resonates, but they receive enough guidance and parameters to make this a successful learning experience. Brigid told me, "Although we provide guidelines and rubrics, many tasks are open-ended, so the students do not limit themselves to what they think we want, and more often than not, I am impressed with what they produce."

For Grace and her peers, this choice was empowering. Grace chose to share her learning in a music video (see Figure 5.5); Julia chose to represent her work in a photo essay (see Figure 5.6).

Another possibility is to prepare an option grid that lists potential project forms in the boxes of the grid and allows students to choose the one that resonates most deeply. The hope is that students will vary their choices across a year and choose one form now and another one later. When I choose to present options in this type of grid (sometimes called a tic-tac-toe planner), I use a three-by-two grid, thus offering only six choices. Figure 5.7 is an example of an option grid, using the choices from the above eighth-grade unit and adding other possible options.

Figure 5.5 Student Music Video*

Allowing choice of topic and/or form provides opportunities for positive decision making, builds independence, and motivates students.

---

*https://www.youtube.com/watch?v=8DwzwC73j1M&feature=youtu.be

Figure 5.6 Student Photo Essay

STUDENT PROJECT CHOICES		
Prezi Presentation	Photographic Essay	Annotated Scrapbook
Annotated Music Video	Brochure	Film (including script)

Figure 5.7 Option Grid Sample

Each choice contains a written and visual element; some are low-tech, some high-tech, and some involve more art or even the element of music. This allows for student readiness, student needs, my discretion, and student interest, thus creating purpose, developing autonomy, and building mastery.

Choice matters. It is what drives us, interests us in learning, and will engage us continuously and consistently in a learning experience. It is a principle of teaching that will lead to the highest level of sustained engagement. When planning your year with students, consider carefully where choice will live inside your teaching!

■ CHOICE CHECKLIST

Choice Applied to Content

☐ Choosing Materials
    ☐ Are students able to choose learning materials?
    ☐ Do these choices allow for differences in need, learning style, and interest?

☐ Mapping Curriculum
    ☐ Does your curriculum include student choice?
    ☐ Is the documentation of this curriculum clear and accessible for all colleagues teaching a grade level, subject, or course?

Choice Applied to Process

☐ Choosing Learning Strategies and Tools
    ☐ Are students able to choose learning strategies?
    ☐ Are students able to choose tools in daily learning situations?
    ☐ Do choices of strategies and tools allow for differences in need, learning style, and interest?

☐ Scheduling Learning Tasks: School and Home
    ☐ Are students able to choose when they can complete in-class and homework assignments?
    ☐ Does this choice reflect students' needs, their home life, and how they spend their personal time?

Choice Applied to Product

☐ Choosing Project Topic
    ☐ Are students able to choose project topics?
    ☐ Is this choice open yet limited enough to ensure sound decisions?

☐ Choosing Project Form
    ☐ Are students able to choose the form of a project?
    ☐ Are these choices similar enough to ensure the same learning outcomes?
    ☐ Do these choices allow for differences in student need, learning style, and interest?

Chapter Six

Engaging Students Through the World Around Them

● ENGAGEMENT THROUGH POPULAR CULTURE

When I began teaching I wasn't much older than my students, so I knew what made them tick. I watched *Friends* and *Seinfeld*; I went Rollerblading on weekends; I even used one-on-one basketball games and World Series parties as rewards for good behavior.

My students responded, not just because it was fun to beat me 5–4 in a basketball game or receive a big wave as they Rollerbladed past my classroom window, but because they knew I understood them. I knew what mattered to them and was able to use this information to engage them in learning.

There is a lot in the world of popular culture that students connect to, and it varies by age, gender, geography, and other factors. The key to using popular culture to cultivate engagement is to think critically about cultural components that resonate with students and will be appropriate and effective ways to engage them in the classroom. Regardless of age, gender, and geography, two areas of popular culture that consistently resonate are technology, including gaming and social media, and popular literature.

Technology

When my daughter was seven, we pulled into the driveway on our mostly calm suburban street and she saw her friend Claire. "Mommy," Rhiannon asked, "can I go across the street to talk to Claire?" "Sure," I replied, then quickly panicked when I realized she didn't know how to cross the street, and that I had never taught her. I could recall being specifically taught how to cross the street. It was a lovely day in the spring of 1973 and my mother was teaching me, a slightly precocious and determinedly independent four-year-old, how to cross the street properly and safely. "Look right first, Tricia, and then look left. Then look one more time to the right. If all is clear and no car is coming, then you can cross over to Uncle Tony" (not actually my uncle, but a neighbor and the father of my across-the-street friends, who was usually waiting on the other side). How remiss it was not to have taught my daughter this important and seminal life skill. How was it that at seven years old she could download her iPod but not cross the street?

Panic and guilt aside, the occurrence was logical. It was 2007, not 1973, and Rhiannon had not once needed to cross the street by herself. However, she quite often wanted to download her iPod. My children's generation and the one before it are digital natives. They grew up using technology every day. As educators, we can embrace that. We have seen how technology has improved our lives and how it has kept us connected and informed in a way we never imagined.

In a study commissioned by Apple Computer, Inc. on technology and student engagement, Judith Haymore Sandholtz, Cathy Ringstaff, and David Dwyer (1994) endorse the use of technology as a way to increase student engagement, which they define as "initiative, self-motivation, independent experimentation, spontaneous collaboration and peer coaching, and enthusiasm or frustration." They found that technology, when used appropriately and integrated into the long-term aspects of curriculum and learning, had positive impacts on student engagement and outcomes:

> The introduction of technology into the classrooms described in this study brought about numerous changes in student engagement. Students displayed increased initiative by going beyond the requirements of assignments, and by independently exploring new applications. The time students spent on assignments and projects increased when they used the computers, and they chose to work on the computers during free time and after-school hours. Students' independent experimentation at the computer led to spontaneous peer coaching and cooperative learning. Increased student enthusiasm facilitated their learning and reinforced the teachers' efforts. The enthusiasm of individual students also motivated other students in the class.

Yet when thinking about how technology can engage and positively impact our students, we sometimes shy away from certain types as distractions. This is natural and not altogether untrue. In *From Fear to Facebook: One School's Journey*, Matt Levinson (2010) writes, "The shift in thinking from fear to Facebook (or opportunity) takes time for school communities to work through, and schools nationwide must steer a new course with technology right there to help navigate the sea change" (5). He also suggests, "But schools also need to draw boundaries for students around issues like chatting, texting, downloading, and gaming, much to the chagrin of freewheeling students, many of whom are accustomed to more lax rules at home surrounding technology." He goes on to tell how his school embraced and included technology more fully into its instruction, practice, and culture and what that journey was like.

We need to take a similar journey. The key is to remember that technology is a tool, a means to an end, not technology for the sake of technology. Just like the sharpened stick, the piece of chalk, the number two pencil, or the dry-erase marker, technology is a tool for learning and should be seen as such.

In an *Education Week* blog interview with Eric Sheninger, author of *Digital Leadership*, Larry Ferlazzo (2014), asks about using technology as a learning tool and letting students bring their own devices to class, wondering how teachers "effectively deal with the nonacademic temptations." Eric explains:

> Our school emphasizes that student-owned devices will be used to enhance learning, increase productivity, and conduct better research. [This] focus . . . has reduced this temptation, but not eliminated it. For change in this area to occur we must recognize that this is not a solely a technology issue as there have always been off-task behaviors prevalent in our schools since the beginning of time. Remember the days when archaic technology in the form of a pencil and paper was used to satisfy the same nonacademic temptations? . . . [P]roper policies, procedures, and support structures must be researched and put in place before adopting a BYOD [bring your own device] initiative. If this is done then BYOD can and will succeed in any school.

A particularly engaging element of technology is gaming, sometimes referred to as *gamification*. Who doesn't like to play a game? We all do and have preferences for the games we like to play. In recent generations, games are less about cards, words, or even outdoor sports, more about gaming via technology. Many teachers use games that are infused in popular culture to engage students in learning. One example is the use of games such as Minecraft. Why Minecraft? When considering gaming and learning, it is important to understand that the game not only should interest students but also should hold potential for engagement and ultimately potential for learning. In Minecraft, there is the ability to increase complexity for the student and the opportunity for students to collaborate. I have seen teachers use Minecraft to teach and practice scale, the formula for volume, and basic algorithms in math; develop depth of understanding of the traits of character and setting in language arts; and practice the skills of geography or demonstrate understandings of a civilization and culture in social studies.

These games should not only resonate with students but also contribute to their learning. In a blog post titled "Four Important Reasons to Pair Mobile Devices with Interactive Whiteboards (and How to Do It!)," Christie Neumann (2014) identifies four key functions of technology in instruction: collaboration, evaluation, demonstration, and engagement. It all comes down to meaning, purpose, and audience. Technology can lead to meaningful learning and, like all learning tools, should achieve a desired purpose for a specific group. The decision to use gaming, and games like Minecraft, is based on providing structures that both challenge students and enable them to collaborate.

Jordon Shapiro (2014) defines gamification as the gaming of elements or aspects of our everyday lives: "In general, gamification attempts to superimpose the stimulating motivational aspects of the game world onto the life world." There are many sites that gamify learning. One is Kahoot (see the screenshot in Figure 6.1), where teachers can take their content and create game-based learning endeavors. Students are able to work toward

Sites like Kahoot bring the elements of gaming to students in interactive and engaging ways.

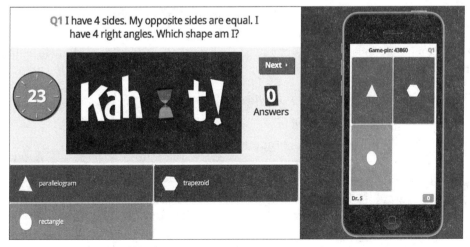

Figure 6.1 Screenshot of Kahoot

mastery of material and build understanding in their own ways, taking ownership of their learning.

Social media are other powerful twenty-first-century tools. Our students use social media every day and need to learn to interact with them in positive and appropriate ways. Something so present and so powerful should be used in the classroom to engage students. What stops us is our fear of the perils. The way to get past the fear is to understand this popular culture tool and use it to cultivate engagement.

Classrooms should have wikis, blogs, Facebook pages, Twitter accounts—whatever builds and sustains community and engagement. We have the option to use the actual social media sites or sites that engage students in using and developing the same competencies and provide the same benefits less publicly. Figure 6.2 lists the social media sites most prevalent in our culture, along with learning possibilities, benefits, and alternatives.

Many teachers use social media effectively and well. When I first began working with Cortney Steffens, she taught first grade. One year, she created a wiki with her students (see the screenshot in Figure 6.3) that proved to be an amazing tool that accomplished many goals. The key is to establish a purpose for the technology. For Cortney and her first graders:

- Students learned how to create and use a wiki.
- They had a digital forum for explaining their thinking and demonstrating their learning.
- The wiki captured a year of learning with and for her students.

She currently teaches third grade and continues to use technology to engage and excite her students. Her class uses class blogs (https://sites.google.com/site/steffens classroomconnections/home) to capture, share, assess, and extend their learning. Students:

- share presentations and projects
- post musings on learning
- respond to posts by other students
- share the responsibility of uploading to and managing the class blog.

Gaming and social media are engaging tools for learning. The key is to use these tools to cultivate and engage students wisely and well. Figure 6.4 list some tenets to follow to achieve this aim.

Social Media	Learning Possibilities	Benefits	Alternative
Facebook/ Instagram	Class Facebook page announcing class events/news Class Facebook page containing pics of student work and projects Student-created Facebook page for fictional or historical characters	Parents and community members keep up with and respond to important events and learning A forum for positive feedback from a real audience Students demonstrate their understanding of a character by posting from the character's point of view	Fakebook (classtools.net) Edmodo
Twitter	Class Twitter page Student-created tweets sharing ideas or demonstrating learning	Parents and community members keep apprised of learning and events Family members get a glimpse into the learning taking place; teachers can base instructional decisions on them	Faketweet (classtools.net)
Blogs	Class blog	Students learn online communication and collaboration tools Parents are kept apprised of student learning	Kid Blogs, Edublogs
Wikis	Class wiki	Students demonstrate their understanding of what they are learning	Wikispaces
Google Classroom	Teacher–student and student–student collaborations	Members of a learning community can collaborate on documents and projects	Google Play for Education account

Figure 6.2 Social Media Chart

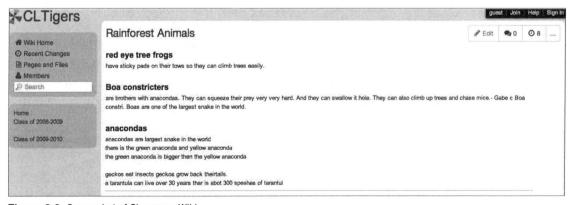

Figure 6.3 Screenshot of Classroom Wiki

Tenet	How It Engages Students
Establish a purpose for the tool.	Purposeful use of technology, including gaming and social media, leads to sustained engagement, not temporary engagement based on novelty.
Make this purpose explicit to students.	When students know the purpose of the technology (collaboration, challenge, evaluation, presentation, etc.) they will use it more skillfully and appropriately.
Find an audience for the tool.	Authentic audience drives purpose and creates a real context for learning. Consider who the audience is and what students will share with this audience.
Instruct students on how to use the tool.	Not all students are adept at using all technology, nor are they adept at using technology for educational purposes. By providing direct instruction in how to use the technology, we ensure proper use, effective outcomes, student ownership, mastery, and sustained engagement.
Minimize distractions.	Engage students in conversations that establish boundaries and ask students to use the technology fairly and honestly. This will minimize distractions and inappropriate use.

Figure 6.4 Tenets for Using Technology Effectively

Popular Literature

Many of us remember staying up until midnight to buy the next Harry Potter book or rushing to catch the first showing of *The Great Gatsby*. My kids loved *Ramona and Beezus*, and my daughter and her friends talked incessantly about Katniss' exploits in the Hunger Games trilogy. Literature engages us. Inside a good story we find our own story, our own voice, our own hopes and dreams, our own struggles. Over the years, countless books, alone or as part of a series, have resonated with our students. What better way to tap into popular culture and connect with our students? (Ways and rationales are summarized in Figure 6.5).

First, and most obviously, we can use these texts as instructional tools: study the change in Harry Potter's character from book one to book four; close-read the scene in which Katniss and Head Gamemaker Plutarch Heavensbee share a dance and Plutarch shows her the watch bearing the image of a mocking jay; compare scenes in *The Great Gatsby* with those in the recent movie version.

We can also build community and collaboration around popular literature. What better way to engage reluctant readers than with the most enticing literature? For our youngest students, it might be reading *The Day the Crayons Quit* by Drew Daywalt to reach them through humor. For our upper elementary students, it might be putting the Little League series by Matt Christopher or *One for the Murphys* by Lynda Mullay Hunt in their hands. For middle school or high school students, it may mean introducing them to edgy and fast-paced novels such as the Maximum Ride series by James Patterson or *Black Ice* by Stephen Tesher.

Students can form book clubs centered on the literature they read and love, perhaps debating the integrity of both good and evil characters or comparing a contemporary dystopian text to an earlier example of the genre (*The Hunger Games* and Shirley Jackson's story "The Lottery," for example). We can use events or ideas from popular books to explore important contemporary or historical events or ideas, perhaps referencing the Hunger Games when exploring the Bill of Rights, civil disobedience, or human empowerment. Or we can use the names of characters or places in these books for elements of our classroom structure: name classroom learning stations or tables after the houses at Hogwarts, or imagine the classroom as a new society with rules and customs similar to the worlds in dystopian novels.

> *Weave popular culture* literature into your classroom to excite and engage students.

Use	Why This Engages Students
Choose popular books as instructional tools.	These texts resonate with students. They invite students into learning a familiar and admired pathway.
Use literature to build community and encourage collaboration.	Good literature builds community and brings students together around common ideas.
Use popular books to explore contemporary or historical ideas or events.	Connections breed engagement. Connecting an engaging element of popular culture to current or historical events leads not only to engagement but to deeper learning.
Incorporate popular characters, settings, or plot elements into classroom structures.	Used this way, these features personalize classroom management.

Figure 6.5 Ways and Reasons Popular Literature Engages Students

● ENGAGEMENT THROUGH COMMUNITY

It takes a village to cultivate engagement. Part of this village comprises parents and caregivers. Another part of the village comprises the businesses, not-for-profit organizations, and individuals who operate and live there. Ways we can cultivate engagement through the community include reading programs, community "adopt a classroom" programs, and direct connections with students' families.

Community Reading Programs

It's early Saturday morning and I'm in the cafeteria of the Camden Street School, in Newark, New Jersey. My colleagues and I are setting up tables of books by grade level, anticipating the kinds of books students will want to read. We arrange them in crates organized by both grade level and genre, covers facing out. We place a sign on each crate indicating the kind of books it contains. Principal Sam Garrison is awaiting a food delivery. This event is part of a program called Literacy Lunch—Food for Thought. It's sponsored by LitLife West Hudson, Hope International, and AmeriCorps, a community effort to improve our students' attitude toward and proficiency with literacy. The goal is to give students and their caregivers lunch, time to read, and a model for building lifelong literacy habits. Reading on a Saturday is not an easy sell. Some students have other obligations on Saturdays, many parents work, and getting to the school can be difficult.

I'm here as a volunteer reader, but I also train the volunteers and introduce them to effective, easy-to-implement literacy strategies. Any time spent with text is beneficial, but if we really want to impact student achievement, engagement, and attitude toward literacy, volunteers and caregivers need to be familiar with strategies for literacy development. Three such strategies are explained in Figure 6.6.

Research supports this kind of programming. In a National Center for Family & Community Connections with Schools document reporting on community engagement programming and the effect it has on communities and student achievement, Anne Henderson and Karen Mapp (2002) summarize the research of Joyce L. Epstein and Mavis G. Sanders (2000):

> To understand the positive effects of family-school collaboration, Epstein developed a new perspective to show that families, schools, and communities have a common mission around children's learning and development (Epstein 1987). This view recognized that home, school, and community act as overlapping spheres of influence on children. Social capital (the benefits of interactions among people) increases when well-designed partnerships enable families, students, and others in the community to interact in productive ways. Social capital may be invested in ways that help students learn, strengthen families, improve schools, and enrich communities. Children grow up in multiple contexts that are connected by a web of networks.

The literacy lunch program brought together volunteers from community organizations in a way that supported students and families, but more importantly, it impacted the ways that students and caregivers interacted outside school. Another way for students and caregivers to interact together inside and outside of school is through celebrations. One such type of celebration is World Read Aloud Day, a global celebration of reading started by LitWorld. Information on how to create a community reading program is available at www.communityplanningtoolkit.org /sites/default/files/Engagement.pdf.

READ ALOUD

Reading aloud to a child is the single most important thing a caregiver or volunteer can do to develop a reader. It models good reading habits and behavior, provides positive reading experiences, develops vocabulary and literary language, and encourages a lifelong love and habit of reading.

When reading aloud, you:

- Establish a context for the reading. Choose the text together and browse it. Look at and comment on the cover (title, author, illustration), notice parts of the book, make predictions about the book, and make connections to the book.
- Read aloud in a clear and engaging voice. Everyone loves a performance!
- Stop at intervals and talk about what is happening. Discuss the plot, information, characters, and so on. Ask questions, but don't quiz your listener. You want this to feel like a conversation.
- After reading, discuss the text. What were your favorite part(s)? Did you learn new or interesting information? Did the ending surprise you? Reread parts or all of the text!

BE THE PERFECT PARTNER

Reading with a child is a way to cultivate a child's reading skills in a friendly and engaging way. A "perfect partner" reads with a child, sharing/dividing the reading and assisting as necessary.

When reading with a child as a perfect partner, you:

- Establish a context for the reading. Choose the text together and browse it. Look at and comment on the cover (title, author, illustration), notice parts of the book, make predictions about the book, and make connections to the book.
- Read with the child in a way that is most comfortable for him or her: alternating pages, having the child "echo" what you read, asking the child to join in on parts or pages (a repeated word, phrase, or sentence, for example).
- Help the child when she or he gets stuck on a word. Encourage the child to look at the picture or parts of the word. If she or he cannot determine the word, say, "Could the word be [such-and-such]?"
- Stop at intervals and talk about what is happening. Discuss the plot, information, characters, and so on. Ask questions, but don't quiz the child. You want this to feel like a conversation.
- After reading, discuss the text. What were your favorite part(s)? Did you learn new or interesting information? Did the ending surprise you? Reread parts or all of the text!
- Accept and praise your reading partner's contributions.

(continues)

(continued)

BE A BOOK CLUB BUDDY

Reading and discussing a text with a child is a powerful way to develop comprehension skills, build student engagement, and encourage a love of different types of texts and genres. A book club buddy reads with but mostly discusses a text with a child in the way of an adult book club. The goal is to talk about and collaborate around the text!

As a book club buddy, you:

- Establish a context for the reading. Choose the text together and browse it. Look at and comment on the cover (title, author, illustration), notice parts of the book, make predictions about the book, and make connections to the book.
- Read with the child in a way that is most comfortable for her or him: alternate pages, simultaneously read parts of the text silently, read aloud.
- Plan how to discuss the text. Think about when you will stop and what kind of conversation you will have.
- Stop at intervals and talk about what is happening. Discuss the plot, information, characters, and so on. Ask questions, but don't quiz the reader. You want this to feel like a conversation.
- After reading, discuss the text. What were your favorite part(s)? Did you learn new or interesting information? Did the ending surprise you? Reread parts or all of the text!
- Reread and/or celebrate favorite parts. Plan your next reading/conversation.

Figure 6.6 Ways to Share Reading

Adopting a Classroom

Members of the larger community can also support student engagement by volunteering in classrooms. During the 2014–2015 school year, I participated in the adopt-a-classroom program at the Camden Street School, in Newark, New Jersey. Assistant principal and director of innovation Meredith Foote reached out to community members for volunteers who would spend time in a classroom each week supporting struggling readers. Although I am an educator by profession, this was by no means a requirement of the program. For these programs to truly cultivate student engagement, the conditions listed in Figure 6.7 should be present. The goal is to interact with students during the school day, caring about them as individuals, supporting their learning, and engaging them as learners.

Making Home–School Connections

Perhaps the most important way to engage students is to develop a connection with their families. Raising a child is hard! There is so much to think about today—both good and bad—that earlier generations didn't have to deal with. We need to make strong positive connections to students' home life by: building relationships, fostering communication, and creating home school initiatives such as a summer reading initiative to bring this about.

CONDITION TO BE MET	RATIONALE
Stress commitment.	Although it wasn't mandatory that I go to my classroom each week, I did. The students, the teacher, and I all looked forward to it. Without this consistency, results will be unpredictable.
Set goals.	The teacher and I set goals for our time together. For me, it was improved reading for students, measured by a formative reading assessment. Goals can focus on student achievement, efficacy, attitude, and so on.
Interact with students directly.	Interaction with students is a must. I spent between sixty and ninety minutes in the classroom working with individual students for twenty or twenty-five minutes each.
Keep records and monitor goals.	I recorded the work I did with students in a Google document (see the example in Figure 6.8) so the teacher and I could then look at these notes together and plan future instruction.
Communicate with teachers and parents.	I also met with the teacher and communicated with parents so everyone was on the same page.

Figure 6.7 Conditions for Effective During-School Programs

5/7/2014

Read words with Telena by picking words from our word jar: *with, at, he, they,* and *no*. She needed to correct each first attempt, and I had to review the long *e* in connection with *he*.

Read *A Rainy Day for Sammy*.

Working on favorite part and retelling.

Misread the title. Did not know Sammy ends in the *e* sound. Talked about the different sounds for *y*.

Excellent picture walk. Talked about beginning, middle, and end of picture walk.

Kept saying *run* for *ran*. Occasionally self-corrected but not always.

Favorite part? My favorite part was when Sammy was running through all the rooms. Why? I liked it. Talked him through that it was funny and he liked how Sammy was getting away from Grant.

Asked him to compose sentences on the whiteboard using the words from the word jar and any other words he needed. He liked composing sentences and worked through quite a few variations (*I, I was*) before he settled on one: *They are at the playgrande*.

Read three titles together and chose two additional books for home reading.

Figure 6.8 Sample Records of Classroom Work

Building Relationships

There are a variety of ways to build connections and build relationships with families. It's important to gather information about each family so we truly understand the home life of the child. When Liz Masi talked with the parents/caregivers of her first graders who were not reading at home, she discovered that many of these homes lacked reading material (one family had recently moved to a shelter). She then initiated a home–school reading program: she sent each child home with a sealed plastic baggie containing three or four books to read that night and a log to be signed by both the student and a caregiver.

However, many teachers are uncomfortable sending books home or investigating why their students are not reading at home. We needn't be. All families regardless of socioeconomic status benefit from conversations about obtaining reading material best suited to their children and setting aside time in the day or evening for their children to read. And in my twenty-five years in education, I can count on one hand the books lost or not returned by students.

Building relationships, through daily interactions or occasional and special check-ins, keep engagement high.

Becoming personally involved in home reading is another possibility. My friend and colleague Sally Rubin-Richards is a reading teacher and literacy coach in Rockland County, New York, who works with struggling readers. When she meets parents and caregivers at the beginning of the year, she explains that she will call their homes periodically and ask to speak with their child, and that she and the child will then read together and discuss what they've read. After each session, Sally either talks with the caregiver or follows up with an email. Students and parents alike are excited when Sally calls, and this connection builds student and family engagement in reading and learning.

Fostering Communication

There are so many ways for educators to communicate today, including a school or classroom Facebook, Twitter, or other social media page and a class Web page. A class Web page is essential: parents and students can find all sorts of engaging information there. (See the home page screenshot of Cortney's class website in Figure 6.9.) The key to using this tool as a method of family engagement is to create a site that is both communicative and interactive.

Another way to engage families is through newsletters and other written communications, printed or digital. The key is to do so with purpose—telling families what their children are learning and giving them opportunities to interact with this

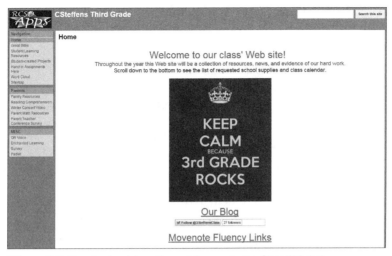

Figure 6.9 Sample of an Interactive and Communicative Class Website*

learning. When I taught fourth grade in Tenafly, New Jersey, every five or six weeks my colleague Anna Reduce and I sent a letter to parents and caregivers asking that they interact with some aspect of student learning—play a math game, study for an assessment, examine their child's portfolio, or visit the classroom. Figure 6.10 is the letter we sent home before the fall parent–teacher conferences.

Parent letters, either print or digital, can inform parents and caregivers of learning in the classroom or create a context for a shared and reflective exercise.

Creating a Summer Reading Initiative

Another opportunity to forge home–school connections is during times the students are not in school during the school year and over the summer. Alicia Eames (2013) explores the impact of summer reading and the disparities in summer reading opportunities for students of different socioeconomic groups in a written interview with Richard Allington. In her introductory remarks, she writes, "Schools sending students off on summer vacation and public libraries gearing up to get kids excited about summer reading programs are both in the business of making sure children become fluent, engaged readers. Unfortunately, the results of those efforts aren't necessarily equal for kids in lower-income situations."

*https://sites.google.com/a/ramapocentral.net/csteffens-third-grade/

November

Dear Parents/Caregivers,

We've been in school for only a few months, yet we have noticed changes and growth in ourselves as learners and as people. It seems only yesterday that we first set goals for ourselves and already it is time to evaluate where we are in reaching them and plan for the next few months. It is also time to share our accomplishments and plans with you.

In preparation for the upcoming parent–teacher conferences, your child and I have selected samples of work depicting the learning taking place in literacy, inquiry, and math and assembled them in two portfolios. The pieces were selected carefully to present a clear and accurate picture of your child as a learner. Along with the samples is a rationale explaining why the particular piece was chosen.

Your child is bringing home his or her portfolio this weekend, before we meet for our conference, and presenting himself or herself to you as a learner. One thing to notice about this working portfolio is that it is a full and "busy" collection that promotes self-analysis, not some tidy showpiece prepared for display. This is the major purpose of portfolios, to develop self-assessors, people concerned about becoming better readers, writers, and thinkers.

Your feedback is very important. After your child has presented her or his portfolio to you, please write her or him a brief letter detailing what you have noticed about his or her growth. Your comments, suggestions, and encouragement are an important part of your child's continued growth and will be extremely helpful as she or he sets goals for the coming months. All portfolios need to be returned to school, with your letters enclosed, by Monday, November 11th.

The children and I are looking forward to sharing with you the goals, the things we have noticed, and the growth we have experienced over the past months.

Best,

Figure 6.10 Sample Parent/Caregiver Letter

Alexander, Olson, and Entwisle (2007) have found that the gap between higher and lower socioeconomic students widens considerably each summer. We need to build family engagement through programming and support during vacations—especially summer reading.

A few years ago I presented this idea to all my partner schools. We began by examining both the negative impact of not reading and the positive impact of reading during the summer months. I then recommended that as a learning community each school create a summer reading protocol that:

1. connected one year of learning to the next and school reading to summer reading

2. included titles of specific texts that matched readers' interests, level, and purpose

3. supported the lending, purchasing, and borrowing of texts for students.

Student engagement is a year-round endeavor, and summer reading is a key component to maintaining student engagement levels.

Figure 6.11 outlines essential components of a summer reading program, along with suggestions for making it manageable.

Essential Component	Management Suggestions
Teachers and students together create a list of summer reading possibilities for each reader that matches reader interest, level, and other pertinent factors (a fall literacy unit, for example).	This personalization doesn't need to be cumbersome. Collaboratively, create lists by grade level that are appropriate for a variety of readers. Then personalize the lists with a particular reader considering their interests or upcoming curriculum element in mind. Text titles will overlap between readers; the key is to create lists of texts that enable them to continue to read long and strong during summer months.
Teachers and readers set goals for when and where reading will take place (see the first grade example in Figure 6.12).	Wrap up the year during the last two weeks of school with a unit on reflection; include time to look back and celebrate the year of learning and set goals for the summer.
Students receive books to take home or are given digital links to them. More often than not, students don't read during the summer because they do not have materials to read.	Enlist local bookstores or public libraries. Send over lists of reading materials and have these facilities order or gather them. Multiple copies of hot titles ensure the maximum number of interested students have access to them. Use school materials. One of my partner schools had a book room with many unused books left over from the days of ordering sets of class novels. We sent them home with students. Approach book publishers. Some have community engagement programs that provide students with books at no cost.
Parents and caregivers participate in the planning through letters, the school website, or social media.	Administrators or other building leaders can compose the appropriate letters or blog posts. At the Dwight-Englewood School, in Englewood, New Jersey, assistant principal Susan Abramson took the lead in communicating reading expectations to parents (see Figure 6.13).

Figure 6.11 Essential Components of a Summer Reading Program and How to Manage It

Figure 6.12 First-Grade Student Sample—Goals for Summer Reading

The Teacher as Engaged Learner

The first time I flew with my now fourteen-year-old daughter, she was a baby, only nine months old. I listened attentively to the flight attendant as she went through the drill of what to do in an emergency and was appalled by the direction that if the oxygen in the cabin dropped I was to put the oxygen mask on myself first, then my child. How could I deny this precious nine-month-old baby oxygen while I was breathing? But then I realized that if I did not give myself oxygen first, I would not be able to care for my child. What at first felt counterintuitive suddenly felt right.

As teachers, we encounter this same phenomenon. We want to be there for our students and for our school community, and sometimes we forget to take care of ourselves. Therefore, when we consider our students' engagement, we need to start with ourselves as engaged learners. We can do this in three ways:

1. Find our teaching passions, the things that will keep us focused and interested as educators.

2. Maintain a rich professional reading and learning life.

3. Create a network of like-minded professionals with whom we can collaborate and commiserate.

Dear Parents,

Each year in the Lower School we have a small assembly on Mr. Rocky's Field to celebrate the end of another year, in particular the fifth graders' transition from the Lower School to the Middle School. Fifth graders plant a tree to commemorate their journey and release butterflies to symbolize their "flight" to a new home. Students naturally experience mixed emotions about leaving the safety of the Lower School, and this important ritual helps them acknowledge their experiences and emotions in a calm, joyful way while preparing them to embrace new ones.

Although this assembly focuses on our fifth graders, our reading and writing curriculum provides a similar experience of reflection and anticipation of what's to come through a unit of study we call Reflection and Celebration. This unit is an opportunity for students in kindergarten through fifth grade to reflect on their work over the course of the year, as well as notice and celebrate how they have grown as readers and writers. As readers, students will think back to their favorite titles and authors and begin to consider the genre they prefer. They will think about the times reading was hard, as well as the times they felt like "strong" readers. They will ask similar questions of themselves as writers, and all students will select a writing piece that will be shared with their next-year teacher. The unit connects one year to the next and gives students and teachers alike time to remember, reflect, and celebrate their shared journey while preparing for the next steps.

As part of their next steps as readers and writers, students make plans for summer reading and writing. Classroom teachers provide students with tools to continue developing their reading and writing identities over the summer. We hope you will encourage your children to write about their summer adventures in words and pictures and to continue reading independently. The attached list includes titles and authors your child and their teacher selected together. These are example of books that will help your child sustain the growth and momentum she or he has worked so hard to achieve all year! We invite you to use these tools, and hope your family will share our commitment to summer reading and writing.

Students entering third through fifth grade are expected to select, read, and bring to school in September one of the books on the suggested reading list. Conversation around these books is part of our work toward building a community of readers in September.

We wish you all the best for a happy and safe summer, one that is filled with lots of memories that will become stories for years to come!

Figure 6.13 Letter to Parents About Summer Reading

Finding Our Teaching Passion—Our *Drishti*

In yoga, when you are trying out poses that require balance, it is helpful to focus on one spot in front of you on the floor, the wall, or some other area. Staring intently at this spot, known as a *drishti*, helps you remain balanced and thus implement and hold the pose.

The same is true of teaching. As educators, we need to find our *drishti*—a focal point or point of interest that keeps us well balanced and positioned. As with our students, this tends to be what interests us most, something about which we are passionate. In today's teaching world, that may seem difficult. There are so many initiatives, mandates, and changes that it is hard to stay focused and find passions. But to be a connected teacher, we need to find the focal point that will keep us engaged in our own teaching and learning.

I do this by identifying a "topic of the year"—a big idea that I am "on about." It can be something large (rethinking my formative assessments or how I use my instructional time) or something smaller (how I wrap up each class period). I started doing this after a conversation I had with my own staff developer, Shirley MacPhillips, in which she commented, "You're interested in so many things!" This isn't a bad thing necessarily, but it didn't lead to productive outcomes. I was constantly switching gears, running from one topic to another, without achieving depth of understanding or clarity.

This doesn't mean that there is only one thing I think and learn about throughout the year or that I am unable to join in when my school or grade-level colleagues or any other community I'm a member of is focusing on a certain topic. It just means I have a teaching *drishti* that keeps me engaged as a learner.

Maintain a Rich Professional Reading and Learning Life

Teachers are and should be readers. We should be well read and well informed, modeling the behavior we want our students to exhibit. Therefore, we need to live full and rich professional reading and learning lives. I do this in three ways:

1. I belong to professional organizations. As a consultant and a teacher I have always belonged to the International Reading Association (IRA), now called the International Literacy Association (ILA), and the National Council of Teachers of English (NCTE), and as a leader, to the Association for Supervision and Curriculum Development (ASCD). Being part of organizations allows me to keep up with what matters most to me and others in education.

2. I attend professional gatherings held by these organizations. I present at conferences, but it is just as important that I participate as an attendee. I

also try to look beyond the usual conferences to new learning ventures. A few years ago, my colleague Jaime Margolies and I attended the Learning Forward conference in Boston for the first time. It was invigorating to attend sessions in a new learning community.

3. I read widely every week, ranging from social media sites such as Twitter to the New York Times to professional magazines and blogs, including *Harvard Education Letter, Educational Leadership* (ASCD), Edutopia posts, *Education Week Teachers College Journal*, the *Marshall Memo*, and the IRA periodicals *Reading Today* and *Reading Research Quarterly*.

These three regular and routine aspects of my life keep me an engaged learner.

Jessica Espinoza and Liz Veneziano, New Jersey school administrators, know how to cultivate professional reading and learning lives. When Jessica and Liz were working together in Emerson, New Jersey, they offered their teachers great professional learning opportunities during the school year and created learning contexts for them each summer as well. One summer, they created a blog on which teachers could post musings about summer reading. Another summer, each teacher launched a Twitter page; tweets from teachers and administrators in this district are among my favorites.

Professional reading and learning can take many forms, but reading and learning every day keeps us growing and engaged.

Find Your Professional Posse

I am a very collaborative person. I am the seventh child in a family of nine; I grew up on a baseball team and enjoy having people to learn and think alongside. I operate from the belief that I will learn something new every day, at work and at home. To that end, I have a group of individuals—my teaching posse—who I turn to when I have questions and ideas.

When I am grappling with a struggling reader, I call Sally. She is my reading friend, the one I talk to about all things reading. When I am thinking about work with my client schools, I call Jaime. Jaime and I have never taught together, but people who have been in both of our classrooms remark on how similar our teaching is. She reminds me of what I value in teaching and helps me think through the particulars of being a coach to many different school communities.

When I want to imagine a new adventure or talk with someone who knows what great teaching looks like, I call Bev: hers is an amazing classroom. She is the one I go to when I want to float an idea or be reminded of what matters most. She and I have recently created a blog together (http://whatmattersmostinteaching.blogspot .com) where we continue to develop and grow ideas together. When I want advice, especially from a leadership perspective, I call Ella. Ella was my principal when I taught in Tenafly, New Jersey, both a colleague and mentor, the person who best knows my teaching. She gives me advice based on her own experience. When I am looking to innovate or start a new project, I call Pam. She and I have worked together for many years, but we began our collaboration decades ago, when she first visited my classroom. She is a kindred spirit.

Some of these women don't know each other, but they have one thing in common: me. They think with me and laugh with me and learn with me and commiserate with me and evolve with me and keep me the most engaged I can be in my learning.

To be the most energized and engaged learner, you need to form your own teaching posse. I recommend the following steps:

1. Identify the people in your teaching and learning life who motivate and engage you. Think about what you love about this learning relationship and what it has to offer you.

2. Name what that person offers you and what you have to offer that person.

3. Look for people outside your school or organization community to learn with and from. You push your thinking when you go outside your daily community.

4. Find ways to interact with these learning buddies. Make space to learn with and from them in person or virtually.

Engagement begins with us. When we recognize this, we start within and build engagement outward to include our learning communities and our students.

ENGAGING STUDENTS THROUGH THE WORLD AROUND THEM CHECKLIST

Engagement Through Popular Culture

☐ Engaging Through Technology

    ☐ Have you considered using gaming to engage students in learning content and in practicing skills?

    ☐ Where can you use gamification and gamelike features to motivate and engage students in lessons and independent practice?

    ☐ What social media will you use to create structures for collaboration, challenge, presentation, and interaction at home and school?

☐ Using Popular Literature

    ☐ What popular culture texts resonate with your students? How can you use a component of the story—the setting, the characters, the theme, the lessons they teach—to engage students?

Engagement Through Community

☐ Community Programs

    ☐ Are there opportunities to engage families in after-school or weekend programs?

    ☐ Can you create a program whereby the larger community can support your students and their learning?

☐ Cultivating Home–School Connection

    ☐ How do you build relationships with families?

    ☐ In what ways, both digital and print, do you communicate with families?

    ☐ How do you support and create summer learning opportunities?

☐ The Teacher as Engaged Learner

    ☐ What are your teaching passions? What can you make your teaching focal point?

    ☐ In what ways are you learning and growing?

    ☐ What professional reading do you do?

    ☐ Who are the colleagues with and from whom you learn the most?

    ☐ What opportunities do you have to learn with and from them?

APPENDIX: A BLUEPRINT FOR A YEAR OF ENGAGEMENT

Strategy/ Principle/Tool	Before the School Year Begins	Early Fall	Late Fall
Creating the Environment	Arrange the physical space in the classroom. Consider furniture arrangement, materials storage, and wall space.	Institute classrooms rituals such as: • daily greetings • weekly class meetings • ritual read-aloud. Introduce materials for managing expectations including: • weekly work checklists • daily "I will" statements • homework routines.	Mix it up! Reattend to the wall space and furniture arrangement. Weed through and remove anchor charts that are no longer pertinent, and consider new seating arrangements. Use what you have gathered about your students as learners to devise new seating. Monitor student self-efficacy: acknowledge risk taking, and celebrate accomplishments!
Setting the Course	Consider the routines that will be essential to the management, flow, and positive tone of the classroom. Create student survey. Create student interview.	Introduce essential routines including: • class meetings • transitions • student talk. Administer student survey. Conduct (or have students conduct) interviews.	Reflect on routines. Are changes needed? Are transitions working?
Assessing Engagement	Gather and copy the student engagement diagnostic assessment.	Fill out the student engagement diagnostic assessment. Create an engagement plan of action for each learner. Introduce the daily appraisals/ engagement checks that will be used across the year including: • checking for understanding routines • entrance/exit tickets • reflection.	Administer a milestone engagement assessment. Revise engagement plan of action if necessary.
Structures of Teaching	Envision how you will use whole-class, small-group, and individual teaching structures.	Introduce the structure of whole-class teaching with students. Model their role in lessons. Incorporate turn and talk and other engagement strategies during the "try" of the lesson. Introduce small-group and one-to-one conferring with students. Model their role in these teaching structures.	Focus on lesson study with an emphasis on lesson timing. Study (perhaps with someone from your teaching posse) the amount of time each part takes, and work toward improving timing to match levels of engagement. Examine your use of engaging materials including visuals. What can be enhanced?

Winter	Spring
Mix it up! Reattend to the wall space and furniture arrangement. Weed through and remove anchor charts that are no longer pertinent, and consider new seating arrangements. Use what you have gathered about your students as learners to devise new seating. Attend to active learning. Incorporate more "can dos" in weekly checklists. Allow students to create the "I will" statements.	Recharge classrooms rituals such as: • daily greetings • weekly class meetings • positive affirmations Monitor growth in student self-efficacy; acknowledge growth and celebrate accomplishments. Set end-of-year goals.
Reflect on essential routines including: • class meetings • transitions • student talk • make adjustments as necessary.	Readminister student survey; document changes and growth.
Administer a milestone engagement assessment.	Administer a milestone engagement assessment. Fill out the student engagement diagnostic assessment. Record growth and changes.
Focus on lesson study with an emphasis on small-group instruction. Is learning differentiated? What types of collaborations can be incorporated into small-group instruction?	Focus on lesson study with an emphasis on one-to-one conferring. Examine the scheduling of conferences and make adjustments as necessary. Cultivate your capacity to use the "perfect partner" strategy in conferences.

APPENDIX: A BLUEPRINT FOR A YEAR OF ENGAGEMENT (*Continued*)

Strategy/ Principle/Tool	Before the School Year Begins	Early Fall	Late Fall
Providing Choice	Consider options for choice. Examine first-quarter/trimester curriculum maps to find choice opportunities.	Build a culture of choice via: • content materials • process • products: consider student choice of project topics.	Integrate choice in the classroom via: • content materials: consider text choice options • process: incorporate student choice for home and school completion of assignments • products.
Engaging Students Through the World: Popular Culture via Literature and Technology	Consider the literature that is current and resonant with students. Imagine where in the year these texts will be integrated into the class community. Design your teacher Web page. Consider the ways that this will be used to: • communicate • collaborate.	Introduce a popular culture tool including: • literature • games or gaming • social media. Introduce technology tools, and make parents partners in safe, appropriate and engaging technology use.	Incorporate gaming or gamelike features into lessons and activities.
Engaging Students Through the World: Self, Parents, the Outside Community	Create family communication routines: engage parents/ caregivers as partners. Consider big ideas that you will study this year: find your drishti.	Communicate class milestones to families via a letter, tweet, or post. Create your short stack of professional texts. Create rituals so that you institute consistent professional reading.	Engage families with a fun and informative family activity such as a literacy night or science share. Check in with someone from your teaching posse!

Winter	Spring
Integrate choice in the classroom via: • content materials: examine winter curriculum and consider options for choice within • process: provide student choice for learning strategies • products.	Integrate choice in the classroom via: • content materials: consider student learning style and incorporate choice of tools • process • products: integrate student choice of product form. Determine choice options for summer work.
Use a popular culture tool. Consider incorporating elements of popular literature throughout the year.	Use a popular culture tool. Consider using a social media tool to capture and share the year's learning.
Communicate class milestones to families via a letter, tweet, or post. Check in with someone from your teaching posse!	Create your short stack of professional texts for summer reading. Create rituals so that you institute consistent professional reading.

Bibliography

Alexander, Karl L., Linda Steffel Olson, and Doris R. Entwisle. 2007. "Lasting Consequences of the Summer Learning Gap." *American Sociological Review* 72 (April): 167–80. www.nayre.org/Summer Learning Gap.pdf.

Allen Simon, Cathy, and Patrick Striegel. "Exit Slips." Strategy Guide. ReadWriteThink. NCTE. Accessed July 5, 2014. www.readwritethink.org/professional-development /strategy-guides/exit-slips-30760.html?main-tab=1#main-tabs.

Anderson, Richard C., Elfrieda H. Hiebert, Judith A. Scott, and Ian A. G. Wilkinson. 1985. *Becoming a Nation of Readers: The Report of the Commission on Reading.* Highlighting Underlining edition. Washington DC: National Academy of Education.

Bandura, Albert, ed. 1997. *Self-Efficacy in Changing Societies.* Cambridge, UK: Cambridge University Press.

Beers, Kylene. 2015. "Motivation." Literacy. Education. Kids. Teachers. Schools. Hope, kylenebeers.com blog post, January 4. http://kylenebeers.com/blog/2015/01/04 /motivation/.

Bray, Barbara. 2012. "10 Steps to Encourage Student Voice and Choice." Rethinking Learning, barbarabray.net blog post, February 3. http://barbarabray .net/2012/02/03/10-steps-to-encourage-student-voice-and-choice/.

Bronson, Po, and Ashley Merryman. 2010. "The Creativity Crisis." *Newsweek*, July 19, p. 45. Accessed May 15, 2014.

Bundick, Matthew J., Russell J. Quaglia, Michael J. Corso, and Dawn E. Haywood. 2014. "Promoting Student Engagement in the Classroom." *Teachers College Record* 116: 1–34. www.tcrecord.org/content.asp?contentid=17402.

Cecil, Bill. 2007. *Best Year Ever! Winning Strategies to ~~Survive~~ Thrive in Today's Classroom.* Wheaton, IL: Best Year Ever! Press.

Collins, Allan, John Seely Brown, and Susan E. Newman. 1987. "Technical Report No. 403 Cognitive Apprenticeship: Teaching the Craft of Reading, Writing, and Mathematics." Accessed July 21, 2015. https://www.ideals.illinois.edu/bitstream/handle/2142/17958 /ctrstreadtechrepv01987i00403_opt.pdf.

Cooper, Kristy S. 2014. "Eliciting Engagement in the High School Classroom: A Mixed-Methods Examination of Teaching Practices." *American Educational Research Journal* (April): 363–402. http://aer.sagepub.com/content/51/2/363.short?rss=1&ssource=mfr.

Csikszentmihalyi, Mihaly. 1998. *Finding Flow: The Psychology of Engagement with Everyday Life*. Mastermind Series ed. New York: Basic Books.

Deci, Edward L., and Richard Flaste. 1996. *Why We Do What We Do: Understanding Self-Motivation*. New York: Penguin.

de Frondeville, Tristan. 2009. "Ten Steps to Better Student Engagement." Edutopia Website, March 11. www.edutopia.org/project-learning-teaching-strategies.

Dennen, Vanessa P., and Kerry J. Burner. 2008. "The Cognitive Apprenticeship Model in Educational Practice." In *Handbook of Research for Educational Communications and Technology: A Project of the Association for Educational Communications and Technology*, 3rd ed., 425–39. Vol. 2 of the AECT Series. New York: Routledge. Accessed July 22, 2014. http://faculty.ksu.edu.sa/Alhassan/Hand%20book%20on%20research%20in%20educational%20communication/ER5849x_C034.fm.pdf.

Denton, Paula, and Roxann Kriete. 2000. *The First Six Weeks of School*. Strategies for Teachers Series. Greenfield, MA: Northeast Foundation for Children and Woodward Design.

Doland, Erin. 2011. "Scientists Find Physical Clutter Negatively Affects Your Ability to Focus, Process Information." Unclutterer blog. http://unclutterer.com/2011/03/29/scientists-find-physical-clutter-negatively-affects-your-ability-to-focus-process-information/.

Dunlap, Joanna C., and Patrick R. Lowenthal. 2010. "Hot for Teacher: Using Digital Music to Enhance Students' Experience in Online Courses." *Tech Trends* 54 (4): 58–59. Accessed July 1, 2014. http://link.springer.com/article/10.1007/s11528-010-0421-4.

Eames, Alicia. 2013. "Summer Reading and the Rich/Poor Achievement Gap: An Educator Responds to Questions." *School Library Journal* Web post, June 4. www.slj.com/2013/06/standards/curriculum-connections/summer-reading-and-the-richpoor-achievement-gap-an-educator-responds-to-questions/#.

Epstein, Joyce L. 1987. "Toward a Theory of Family-School Connections: Teacher Practices and Parent Involvement." In *Social Intervention: Potential and Constraints*, edited by K. Hurrelmann, F. X. Kaufmann, and F. Lasel, 121–36. New York: Walter de Gruyter.

Epstein, Joyce L., and Mavis G. Sanders. 2000. "Connecting Home, School, and Community: New Directions for Social Research." In *Handbook of the Sociology of Education*, edited by Maureen T. Hallinan, 285–306. New York: Kluwer Academic/Plenum Publishers.

Fencl, Heidi, and Karen Scheel. 2005. "Engaging Students." *Journal of College Science Teaching* (August): 20. www.nsta.org/publications/news/story.aspx?id=50829.

Ferlazzo, Larry. 2014. "'Digital Leadership': An Interview with Eric Sheninger." Classroom Q&A. *Education Week Teacher* Web post, August 6. http://blogs.edweek.org/teachers /classroom_qa_with_larry_ferlazzo/2014/08/digital_leadeship_an_interview_with_eric _sheninger.html.

———. 2014. "Response: Differentiating Lessons by 'Content, Process, or Product.'" *Education Week* blog post, April 18. http://blogs.edweek.org/teachers/classroom_qa _with_larry_ferlazzo/2014/04/response_differentiating_lessons_by_content_process _or_product.html.

Fisher, Douglas. n.d. "A Gradual Release of Responsibility." www.glencoe.com/glencoe _research/Jamestown/gradual_release_of_responsibility.pdf.

Fisher, Douglas, and Nancy Frey. 2008. "Homework and the Gradual Release of Responsibility: Making Student 'Responsibility' Possible." *English Journal* 98 (2): 40–45. Accessed July 1, 2014. http://fisherandfrey.com/uploads/posts/Homework_EJ.pdf.

———. 2011. "Checking for Understanding." *Instructional Leader* (September): 60–62. www.nassp.org/Content/158/PLSept11_instructldr.pdf.

Gammill, Deidra. 2014. "'Google Thursdays' and the Power of Self-Directed Learning." *Education Week Teacher* (July 9). www.edweek.org/tm/articles/2014/07/09/gammill _ctq_google.html?cmp=ENL-EU-MOSTPOP.

Glaser, Robert. 1989. "Cognitive Apprenticeship: Teaching the Crafts of Reading, Writing, and Mathematics." In *Knowing, Learning, and Instruction: Essays in Honor of Robert Glaser*. Hillsdale, NJ: Erlbaum.

Guthrie, John T., Allan Wigfield, Pedro Barbosa, Kathleen C. Perencevich, Ana Taboada, Marcia H. Davis, Nicole T. Scafiddi, and Stephen Tonks. 2004. "Increasing Reading Comprehension and Engagement Through Concept-Oriented Reading Instruction." *Journal of Educational Psychology* 96 (3): 403–23. www.corilearning.com/research -publications/2004-guthrie-wigfield-etal.pdf.

Hardiman, Mariale, and Glenn Whitman. 2014 "Assessment and the Learning Brain: What Research Tells Us." *Independent School* (Winter). www.nais.org/Magazines-News letters/ISMagazine/Pages/Assessment-and-the-Learning-Brain.aspx.

Harvey, Stephanie, and Harvey Daniels. 2009. *Comprehension & Collaboration: Inquiry Circles in Action*. Portsmouth, NH: Heinemann.

Haymore Sandholtz, Judith, Cathy Ringstaff, and David C. Dwyer. 1994. "Student Engagement: Views from Technology-Rich Classrooms." Apple Computer, Inc. www .apple.com/nl/images/pdf/acotlibrary/rpt21.pdf.

Henderson, Anne T., and Karen L. Mapp. 2002. "A New Wave of Evidence: The Impact of School, Family, and Community, Annual Synthesis." National Center for Families and Community Connections with Schools, Southwest Educational Development Laboratory, Web post, January 1. www.sedl.org/connections/resources/evidence.pdf.

Hunter, Madeline. 1982. *Mastery Teaching: Increasing Instructional Effectiveness in Elementary, Secondary Schools, Colleges and Universities.* Thousand Oaks, CA: Corwin.

Intervention Central. n.d. "School-Wide Strategies for Managing . . . OFF-TASK / INAT-TENTION." Accessed July 22, 2014. http://www.interventioncentral.org/behavioral-interventions/challenging-students/school-wide-strategies-managing-task-inattention.

Irvin, Judith L., Julie Meltzer, and Melinda S. Dukes. 2007. *Taking Action on Adolescent Literacy: An Implementation Guide for School Leaders.* Alexandria, VA: ASCD.

Jensen, Eric. 2005. *Teaching with the Brain in Mind.* Alexandria, VA: ASCD.

———. 2008. *The New Paradigm of Teaching: Brain Based Learning.* Thousand Oaks, CA: Corwin.

Kush, Joseph, and Marley Watkins. 1996. "Long-Term Stability of Children's Attitudes Toward Reading." *Journal of Educational Research* 89 (5): 315–19. www.bwgriffin.com/gsu/courses/edur9131/content/Reading_Attitudes_Kush_Watkins_1996.pdf.

Leinhardt, Gaea, C. Weidman, and K. M. Hammond. 1987. "Introduction and Integration of Classroom Routines by Expert Teachers." *Curriculum Inquiry* 17 (2): 135–74. http://gaining.educ.msu.edu/resources/files/Leinhardt1987Introduction.pdf.

Levinson, Matt. 2010. *From Fear to Facebook: One School's Journey.* Eugene, OR: International Society for Technology in Education.

Lopez, Shane T. 2014. "Not Enough Students Are Success-Ready." *Gallup Business Journal* April 10. http://businessjournal.gallup.com/content/168242/not-enough-students-success-ready.aspx.

Marciano, Paul. 2012. "Motivation vs. Engagement." YouTube video. Posted by Legacy Business, January 9, 2012. https://www.youtube.com/watch?v=1PeiUT81KPY

Margolis, Howard, and Patrick P. McCabe. 2006. "Improving Self-Efficacy and Motivation: What to Do, What to Say." *Intervention of School and Clinic* 41 (4): 218–27. http://uqu.edu.sa/files2/tiny_mce/plugins/filemanager/files/4340129/4_Improving_Self-Efficacy.pdf.

Marzano, Robert J., Barbara B. Gaddy, Maria C. Foseid, Mark P. Foseid, and Jana S. Marzano. 2008. *A Handbook for Classroom Management That Works.* Alexandria, VA: ASCD.

Neumann, Christie. 2014. "Four Important Reasons to Pair Mobile Devices with Interactive Whiteboards (and How to Do It!)." Tierney Brothers, Inc. blog post, April 17. www.tierneybrothers.com/AboutUs/NewsBlog/4ImportantReasonstoPairMobileDeviceswithInteractiveWhiteboardsandHowtoDoIt.aspx.

Palmisano, Samuel J. 2010. "Capitalizing on Complexity." CEO survey. January 1. Accessed July 28, 2014. www.inspireimagineinnovate.com/PDF/Capitalizing-on-Complexity-IBM-Study.pdf.

Patall, Erika A., Harris Cooper, and Jorgianne Civey Robinson. 2008. "The Effects of Choice on Intrinsic Motivation and Related Outcomes: A Meta-Analysis of Research Findings." *Psychological Bulletin* 134 (2): 270–300.

Pearson, P. David, and G. Gallagher. 1983. "The Gradual Release of Responsibility." *Contemporary Educational Psychology* 8: 112–23.

Pearson, P. David, and Meg Gallagher. 1983. "The Instruction of Reading Comprehension." *Contemporary Educational Psychology* 8: 317–344.

Petrash, Jack. 2002. *Understanding Waldorf Education: Teaching from the Inside Out.* Lewisville, NC: Gryphon House.

Pink, Daniel. 2013. "Compliant Students or Engaged Students, Pick One." Student Engagement Series. Podcast, BAM! Radio. Accessed March 29, 2014. http://pulse.bamradionetwork.com/featured-guest-dan-pink/radio.

Powell, Shawn, and Brett Nelson. 1997. "Effects of Choosing Academic Assignments on a Student with Attention Deficit Hyperactivity Disorder." *Journal of Applied Behavior Analysis* 30 (1): 181–83. www.ncbi.nlm.nih.gov/pmc/articles/PMC1284033/pdf/9103995.pdf.

Provenzano, Nicholas. 2014. "Ending on an Upswing." Edutopia, edutopia.org blog post, June 10. www.edutopia.org/blog/ending-on-an-upswing-nick-provenzano.

Quate, Stevi, and John McDermott. 2009. *Clock Watchers: Six Steps to Motivating and Engaging Disengaged Students Across Content Areas.* Portsmouth, NH: Heinemann.

Reger, Adam. 2013. "Student Engagement More Complex, Changeable Than Thought." University of Pittsburgh News Services website, June 20. http://www.news.pitt.edu/news/student-engagement-essential-success-school-more-complex-changeable-previously-though.

Ryan, Richard M., and Edward L. Deci. 2000. "Intrinsic and Extrinsic Motivations: Classic Definitions and New Directions." *Contemporary Educational Psychology* 25: 54–67.

Sapon-Shevin, Mara. 2010. *Because We Can Change the World: A Practical Guide to Building Cooperative, Inclusive Classroom Communities.* Thousand Oaks, CA: Corwin.

Shalaway, Linda. 1998. *Learning to Teach . . . Not Just for Beginners: The Essential Guide for All Teachers.* New York: Scholastic.

Shapiro, Jordan. 2014. "Tapping into the Potential of Games and Uninhibited Play for Learning." Mind/Shift website blog post, April 22. http://blogs.kqed.org/mindshift /2014/04/tapping-into-the-potential-of-video-games-and-uninhibited-play-for -learning-education/.

Sheninger, Eric C. 2014. *Digital Leadership: Changing Paradigms for Changing Times.* Thousand Oaks, CA: Sage Publications.

Strean, William B. 2011. "Creating Student Engagement? HMM: Teaching and Learning with Humor, Music, and Movement." *Creative Education* 17: 189–92. http://file.scirp .org/Html/6798.html.

Tanner, Kimberly D. 2013. "Structure Matters: Twenty-One Teaching Strategies to Promote Student Engagement and Cultivate Classroom Equity." *CBE—Life Sciences Education* 12: 322–31. www.lifescied.org/content/12/3/322.full.pdf+html.

Thall, T., and Ramona Shawana. 2012. "The Classroom Environment." A Classroom Full of Curiosity and Wonder . . . blog. Accessed October 22, 2014. https://aclassroomfullof curiosityandwonder.wordpress.com/2012/09/08/48/.

Tomlinson, Carol Ann. 2014. *The Differentiated Classroom: Responding to the Needs of All Learners*, 2d ed. Alexandria, VA: ASCD.

Toshalis, Eric, and Michael J. Nakkula. 2012. "Motivation, Engagement, and Student Voice." Students at the Center Website. April 1. www.studentsatthecenter.org/sites /scl.dl-dev.com/files/field_attach_file/Exec_Toshalis&Nakkula_032312.pdf.

Wagner, Tony. 2010. *The Global Achievement Gap: Why Even Our Best Schools Don't Teach the New Survival Skills Our Children Need—and What We Can Do About It.* New York: Basic Books.

———. 2012. "Authors@Google: Change Leadership: Transforming Education for the 21st Century." Video Transcript, March 8. http://transcriptvids.com/v/E4DTaTd8_nE.html.

Wang, Ming-Te, and Jacquelynne S. Eccles. 2013. "School Context, Achievement Motivation, and Academic Engagement: A Longitudinal Study of School Engagement Using a Multidimensional Perspective." *Elsevier Learning and Instruction* 28: 12–23. www.sciencedirect.com/science/article/pii/S0959475213000327.

Washor, Elliot, and Charles Mojkowski. 2014. "Student Disengagement: It's Deeper Than You Think." *Phi Delta Kappan* (May 1): 8–10.